Lobster Rolls

OF

NEW ENGLAND

Seeking Sweet Summer Delight

SALLY LERMAN
The Lobster Gal

AMERICAN PALATE

Published by American Palate
A Division of The History Press
Charleston, SC 29403
www.historypress.net

First published 2014

Manufactured in the United States

ISBN 978.1.62619.408.3

Library of Congress CIP data applied for.

Dedicated to the memory of my grandmother, Barbara Putman Clarke Bannowsky, the woman who introduced me to all the best things in life, including New England and lobster.

Contents

Introduction and Standards

As far as I am concerned, the lobster roll might be the finest food ever assembled. Lobster on its own is certainly one of the best foods, particularly when it is cooked fresh, directly from the sea. It's like eating summer vacation—in New England, anyway. But let's be honest. A fresh cooked lobster, for the full experience, requires that you get your hands dirty—really dirty. I just don't like getting my hands so dirty and possibly bloody (since I'm actually not particularly adept at lobster extraction methods). Much like exercise, while I like the end result, I just can't be bothered with the difficult part. So for those of us lobster lovers who are prissy, lazy and/or impatient, there is life's sweetest gift: the lobster roll. No work, no wait and no mess—it's a lazy man's lobster dinner.

When I first tried a lobster roll, I assumed that every lobster roll was this exact dream come true. Sadly, that is not what all lobster roll purveyors in New England seem to think a lobster roll should be. That is why I made it my life's mission to try every lobster roll in New England—and maybe beyond—and specifically document and report back to the world which lobster rolls live up to the true ideal of fresh picked lobster meat, right out of the shell, served on a bun for handheld convenience.

It was probably my destiny that the very first lobster roll I tried was at the Clam Shack in Kennebunkport, my very favorite lobster roll on the face of the earth (more on that in the Clam Shack's section). But my first experience made many lobster

Fishermen's Grill lobster rolls. *Photo by Sally Lerman.*

rolls disappointing and left me feeling like I had wasted money, time and stomach space. I want to save others from the same fate by pointing them in the direction of the greats. I hope this compilation serves that purpose. I was not able to include every lobster roll that I consider great, so if you see your favorite missing, don't think it was necessarily because I don't think it's great. Although, in fairness, it might have been left out because it didn't meet my personal standards.

I had worked incognito sampling, documenting and photographing lobster rolls for years before I started my blog, lobstergal.com, in January 2012 to share my information with the world. I found it frustrating that so few lobster roll reviews listed useful, objective statements about the roll. What is ideal in a lobster roll is different for everyone, so I provide as much detail as I can so that it might help someone find that perfect lobster roll. I knew my nutrition science degree would come in handy one day; applying the scientific method to the assessment of lobster rolls is like a research project, but delicious. I anonymously visited and documented every location in this book at least once before I approached them for in-depth interviews. I didn't identify myself until after I had ordered, eaten, documented and, most importantly, enjoyed a lobster roll. I will give you my standards of a great lobster roll

Footbridge lobster roll with Ginger, dearly departed canine assistant. *Photo by Sally Lerman.*

to be clear on my perspective. I hope that my information can help everyone find his or her favorite lobster roll. Every lobster roll in this guide is top quality and worthy of being considered anyone's fave.

Fresh Picked Lobster Meat

Every venue in this guide has told me that it always and only uses fresh picked meat and that it never uses frozen meat—ever. I feel this is the one thing that all lobster roll lovers should agree on as an essential component of a great lobster roll. Sure, you might think this goes without saying, just as I did when I first started. But then I found out that lots of places (more than you would ever guess), even many that steam lobsters on site for dinners, actually use previously frozen lobster meat in their lobster rolls. I have actually tasted some rather decent previously frozen meat, but if you are on the New England seaside, in sight of lobster boats in the summer, nothing but fresh is acceptable to me. It should be cooked in-house for the venue to be able to take full credit for the greatness of its lobster roll. However, I understand there are limitations, and as the lobster roll king, Steve Kingston of Clam Shack, says, "If you use only fresh picked meat, you can always hold your head high."

Finding out this sort of intel is no easy feat. Understandably, most places don't want to admit to and certainly don't want to advertise that they are using previously frozen meat. I toyed for years with the best way to find this out. I used to ask, "Is the meat in the lobster roll fresh picked?" But somehow what they heard was, "Is the meat in the lobster roll rotten?" So I have settled on, "Do you use previously frozen meat at all in your lobster roll?" I'm usually asking a gal at the counter who has no idea, but that question might flag her to ask someone in the kitchen or a manager.

Fresh picked meat requires a great deal of ongoing labor compared to packaged, previously frozen meat, which runs about half the price. However, I have noticed consistently that the price for previously frozen rolls is rarely less than that of the fresh rolls. To me, this feels somewhat misleading, as does using a mix of fresh and frozen meat. I understand that some places might use some occasional frozen meat to minimally round out their supply. But since I will never know the specific

Cooking at the Clam Shack. *Jane Shauck Photography*.

proportions, saying they use a mix of fresh and frozen could also mean that they use an extremely minimal amount of fresh meat simply to say so.

I almost always prefer a lobster roll that contains tail meat. In the absence of being able to find out if a lobster roll uses previously frozen meat, the inclusion of tail meat is a good indicator of its freshness. A lack of tail meat also usually indicates to me that the meat was not picked in-house. If there is only claw and knuckle meat on the roll, what did they do with the tail meat (especially if I don't see it in use anywhere else on the menu)? Tail meat is also more prized and expensive than just claw and

Clam Shack
lobster meat.
*Jane Shauck
Photography.*

knuckle meat, even when fresh picked. Each part of the lobster, claw, knuckle and tail has a different texture and flavor. In order to get the lazy man's lobster dinner experience, I need the whole thing.

Another thing I have learned is that just because a lobster is live doesn't mean it is fresh. A live, hard-shell lobster will survive for months out of the sea. But once that lobster is caught, it won't eat again before it is killed. Lobsters can lose quite a bit of weight, not to mention flavor, sitting around in a tank and wasting away for months. I heard once that if there is a thick black vein in the tail and visible tomalley (the green stuff inside the body), it's likely that lobster was swimming wild and free not long ago.

Hard shell versus soft shell is another issue with live lobsters. A soft-shell lobster results when a lobster molts its shell to make room for growth, usually peaking in late summer/early fall. The shell of a soft-shell lobster is the consistency of snow crab legs—you can easily break it with your hands; no need for tools. You get more meat per pound from a hard-shell lobster (as the price reflects) because the shell is filled to the edge with lobster, whereas the soft-shell variety has space in between. Most places in New England that use freshly caught lobsters in their lobster rolls in the summer use exclusively soft-shell lobster. They are easier to pick, far more abundant and have a more tender texture, which works well for a sandwich. As far as the flavor goes, without exception, every lobsterman I spoke to preferred the flavor of soft shell. They say it is more tender and sweeter and that the additional seawater between the meat and the shell brines the meat to give it the superior flavor. The downside is that they don't travel well or live outside of the wild for long; in fact, they rarely leave New England. In lobstering, being able to ship a lobster to Europe or elsewhere and have it live through the trip is essential to the business. Once a lobster dies, it releases toxins and can't be eaten. Cooking must be done while the lobster is alive.

Bread

If you've ever had a lobster roll, you know that the benchmark for bread is generally considered to be a New England top-split hot dog bun. I've never heard self-professed "foodies" so enthusiastic about mass-produced white bread as they are when talking about lobster rolls. It seems a general consensus that in order to be considered a lobster roll, it has to be in such a bun. On this point, I strongly disagree. I feel that lobster, the king of foods, deserves a better vessel than what the boozy, late-night convenience store hot dog receives. And I say this as a person who genuinely enjoys the occasional convenience store hot dog.

A bakery-fresh bun is the only way to go. New England is full of many great local bakeries that should be more heavily utilized by the lobster roll industry. There are most certainly variations in the appropriateness of each individual bun for use with lobster meat. But any attempt at an innovative bun is superior to the "standard" supermarket bun. It did break my heart to hear that a few restaurant owners who tried to use bakery fresh buns got so many complaints that they had to go back to the standard. People are crazy. If you are in this group, I strongly encourage you to try some of the lobster rolls that use great bread and see how good it can be. However, the use of the standard bun is so common that I don't take off points; I simply add points on the rare occasion that I encounter a bakery fresh bun.

If a bun is grilled, it should be grilled in salted butter to a light crispness—exactly the way a good grilled cheese sandwich would be. I find nothing worse than biting into a lobster roll only to have the roof of my mouth mutilated by an overly crisp roll. I know this is not a widely held view on lobster roll bread, but I actually enjoy an un-grilled, un-heated bun.

Opposite: Lobstering with Footbridge Lobster. *Jane Shauck Photography*.

Butter versus Mayonnaise and Hot versus Cold

When I first started this quest, I came down strongly on the side that all lobster rolls should be hot and buttered. It is the standard start for anyone hoping for a lazy man's lobster on bread. I have since come to decide that to make hot and buttered great is extremely difficult. The problem is that lobster meat is already cooked, usually to the ideal consistency. Trying to re-heat it essentially overcooks the meat. I have also found that heating the butter usually results in separated, runny butter that doesn't stick to the meat and soaks through the bread so that the meat falls out of the bottom when you pick up the lobster roll. It is not an easy feat, even when doing it at home on your own. A cold roll is easier and more likely to result in tender lobster meat that is perfectly cooked. When done ideally, to me, the bun is just hot enough to heat the meat up to room temperature, allowing the mayo or butter to just barely melt onto the meat. I feel that any use of mayonnaise should be minimal—you should taste the lobster meat, not mayo, in every bite. In the end, the version I have grown to love best is cold meat glossed with just enough mayo to keep it all in the bun, which has been grilled to heat the whole thing up. Then I like to dip each bite in a cup of melted butter for pure perfection—as long as the meat doesn't fall out. So I suppose my answer is all four: hot, cold, butter and mayo.

Size and Weight

Being large in and of itself is not necessarily a virtue. Most extremely large lobster rolls use previously frozen lobster meat or an undisclosed mixed ratio of frozen and fresh. I have, however, never met a fresh picked lobster roll that I considered to be too big. I never take anyone's word for it that a lobster roll is huge. I carry my trusty scale with attached measuring tape to assess the real size of a lobster roll. A lobster roll looking big and weighing in as big are two very different things—the eyes can deceive. The weight I take is that of the entire finished lobster roll, which takes into account mayo, butter and bread density. Thus, a naked lobster meat roll probably has more meat than a heavily mayonnaised lobster roll weighing the same.

All weights were taken on my digital scale and then again on my analog scale to see if there were differences due to uneven picnic tables and other less-than-ideal weighing conditions. Some do not include a weight because I visited them before I incorporated weighing and didn't feel it would be a fair comparison to weigh the photo-ready interview roll against the incognito reviewed rolls.

I also look for chunk size. Ideally, I prefer entirely uncut lobster meat—just a tail, split in half to be deveined, and the lobster claws and knuckles as nature intended. However, I have recently come to see the value in a mix of chunks and shreds. The greater surface area allows for more cohesion of the meat, allowing it to stay in the bun more efficiently.

My scales are not official or calibrated, so don't take the weights too seriously; they are included mainly to give an idea of relative size.

"Spongies"

I don't know that I invented this word to describe lobster, but I don't know that I didn't. "Spongies" are the "fingers" of the lobster, the wispy pieces attached to the round claw that are usually spongy in texture and gross me out. I tend to feel that they are like the vein and should be removed before consumption. There are a few exceptions to this rule. In flawlessly cooked lobster, which I have encountered only a handful of times, the spongies have a more flexible, slippery texture, and I almost enjoy them. The mark of true lobster perfection is when the spongies are included and I don't mind.

Anything Else

Salt, pepper and fresh lemon are very acceptable and usually quite good on a lobster roll. Lettuce, celery or anything else is generally frowned upon. I say "generally" because there are some top chefs capable of real fantastic innovation using unexpected ingredients—Eventide Oyster Co. comes to mind. Whole leaf lettuce doesn't bother me because it is easy to pick off. I'm not a fan of lettuce shreds because you can't pick them off, but a small amount can actually be good. Celery is only OK with me if it is at the peak of summer freshness and is minced to a size that just melts into the lobster meat, adding a hint of freshness. Anything bigger than finely minced is not for me.

Price

I rarely mention specific prices. I find that although it fluctuates frequently, prices are usually between fifteen and twenty dollars. You may have heard that lobster rolls are overpriced. Those articles are usually based on the soft-shell price that lobstermen are getting directly from selling it to the lobster wharf. It in no way accounts for the die off of soft-shell lobsters, transport, distribution and storage, not to mention the labor involved in cooking and picking meat that can be used only for that one day. It is also a seasonal product, available in abundant supply only three months out of the year. You are paying for labor, and if you ever watched the process from beginning to end, you would know that most any price they charge is still an excellent deal.

View of the sunset from Boothbay Lobster Wharf. *Photo by Sally Lerman.*

Open Season

Open season is listed for every establishment, but I strongly suggest you call ahead if you're planning a trip because hours and seasons can vary widely. I have shown up at places only to find that they closed for the season the day before.

Happy lobster roll trails to you!

CHAPTER 1

Sea to Table

There are still very few things we eat that were living out in the wild in their natural state, as the good Lord intended, just hours before we eat them. The lobster roll, particularly when eaten on the New England coast, is one of those things. Many lobster rolls in this book didn't travel even as far as some of the fruits and veggies at your local farmers' market did to get from the source to you.

We were able to stand out on the small dock in the middle of Cape Porpoise Harbor and watch the catch come in with Eric Emmons, the lobsterman and wharf owner who sources lobsters directly to Clam Shack. The lobstermen drop off their catch and are paid right there. I love to get lobster rolls from a lobsterman or lobster wharf so that the majority of the price of the lobster roll is going to the people who are working out on the water. It also means that the lobster roll is absolutely as fresh as they come.

The locavore movement is all about supporting your local farmers. Sure, you might think lobstermen aren't farmers, but that's not how Chris Eager, lobsterman and owner of Footbridge Lobster in Ogunquit, sees it. Jane Shauck and I had the privilege of heading out on the high seas with Chris and Tristin Boyd on the *Miss Mae* one October morning. We quickly forgot that it was the middle of the night and we hadn't had a drop of coffee as we took in the magic that they get to see every day. Standing on the dock on Badger's Island in Kittery, Maine, we were able to see

Above: Footbridge's *Miss Mae*. *Jane Shauck Photography*.

Below: Clam Shack's Eric Emmons. *Jane Shauck Photography*.

the city of Portsmouth, New Hampshire, sound asleep with some lights marking the activity of the world waking up on the water. They loaded up the bait (sparing our girly noses some of the smellier bait they generally bring along), Tristin sharpened his fishing knife and we headed out. Everything lit up from the reflections off the water long before the sun came up, so when Chris pointed out that the sun was rising, I was genuinely surprised it hadn't risen already.

Chris and Tristin keep over eight hundred traps and spend the day hauling them in about ten at a time. To maintain a healthy lobster population, the laws in Maine require lobstermen to throw back lobsters that are smaller than about a pound or larger than about four pounds, as measured by their body size. If the lobster's tail has been notched, it is an egg-bearing female and must be thrown back as well. If they catch a lobster with eggs on her tail, she gets notched and thrown back to live a long egg-bearing life. The Maine lobster trap fishery is certified

Footbridge's Tristin Boyd. *Jane Shauck Photography*.

as sustainable to the standard of the Marine Stewardship Council, according to www.seafoodwatch.org.

When I expressed concern to Chris that they seemed to be throwing back nearly all of the lobsters in the traps and that their bait was always eaten, he explained to me that he considers lobstermen to be the farmers of the sea. The way he sees it, they are feeding their crop, and that keeps the harvest strong. He actually sees it as a bit of a life mission to teach children about where the lobsters come from. One way he accomplishes this is through the television at Footbridge, which streams a live feed from the boat showing exactly what a lobstering day looks like.

We learned of the danger associated with this profession when they asked us to stand well out of the way as the traps on the rope went back into the water. We thought it was just because we would be in the way, but Tristin explained why all lobstermen carry knives. The line of lobster traps might be moving slowly, but it is headed straight for the bottom with no way to haul the traps back up as they are falling. If the rope gets wrapped around your ankle, as happened to Tristin's brother once, you head straight down. Luckily, Tristin was able to dive in after his brother and cut the rope to save him. In typical casual lobstering fashion, he says, "He cried a little, but he was fine." But his brother spent time in the hospital and never lobstered again.

Love and hard work are really what go into a lobster roll. These men and women seem to love the work they do. I was able to see the entire process, which entails heading out at 4:00 a.m. to haul in the traps and then spending the afternoon selling and then delivering fresh lobster. The folks at lobster roll places start their days very early as well, cooking and picking all of that lobster meat. Experiencing the entire orchestration that results in fresh picked lobster rolls— even just for the brief glimpse I was able to get—made me truly appreciate that New England sea-to-table experience.

CHAPTER 2

History of the Lobster Roll

PERRY'S—THE BEST LOBSTER ROLL WE'LL NEVER EAT

A great deal of mystery surrounds the history of the lobster roll. We know that lobster was being eaten in New England as far back as the Pilgrims, but at what time someone decided to make a sandwich out of it is anyone's guess. From speaking to many lobster roll purveyors about what they know of the history of the lobster roll and when they started serving them, I have come up with a few theories of my own. It seems that cold lobster meat between two slices of bread (sometimes with mayonnaise) has been eaten in coastal Maine for as long as anyone can remember. I heard stories that during the Depression, children would bring lobster salad sandwiches to school for lunch and hide when they ate them because it was a sign that they were poor. I guess the rich kids got peanut butter and jelly.

It seems that selling lobster rolls in New England really started to become popular around the 1970s. Few people remember them being sold—and certainly not as being particularly popular—until more recent times. There was one place that seems to be the undisputed originator of the idea of selling a hot lobster roll: Perry's in Milford, Connecticut. I would say Perry's invented the lobster roll as we know it, but as it turns out, the original is nothing like anything seen today.

It was the great thrill of my lobster roll–stalking life to be able to actually speak with Wendy Weir, the granddaughter of the inventor of the hot lobster roll, Harry Perry, and to have her share with me, for the first time publicly, the exact method used to make the original lobster roll.

Harry Perry's family had a house on Gulf Pond in Milford, and they ran a seafood market there for years. They later expanded into a small, casual "roadhouse-style" restaurant, as Wendy describes it, serving fried seafood and beer. One day in the 1920s, a salesman came into Perry's restaurant and wanted lobster, but he didn't want a whole lobster, so Harry put together a grilled lobster sandwich for him. It soon became the most popular item on the menu, and Harry trademarked the "Hot Lobster Roll" in 1929. He didn't get a patent because at the time, food patents needed to change only one small ingredient to be considered different.

The bun was specially crafted by French's Bakery in Bridgeport and delivered fresh every day. It was similar to a white-bread hot dog bun but larger and denser in texture. Here is the part that blew my mind. Wendy says, "I hear top-split roll, top-split roll—that's really the shortcut way of doing it. That's not the way we did it at all." They actually notched a "V" out of the center by cutting in along the length of the roll at an angle on both sides, making a kind of sandwich boat. The top "V" was removed, and both sides of the inside "V" were buttered.

The lobsters were cooked and picked fresh every day by the Perrys. They cut the tail meat into chunks and shredded the claws and knuckles. I have since come to believe that this might be the ideal way of making a lobster roll because it gives lots of surface area for the butter and allows it to stick to the bun and hold the whole thing together while still being full of chunks of meat. The meat was then placed in the V-shaped buttered bread boat, and the V-shaped buttered bread lid was placed on top. They would make them up ahead of time and grill them to order.

The cooking process was the most unique aspect, as the sandwich was placed on a sandwich press. Unlike most lobster rolls we see today, the crust sides, not

Perry's lobster roll attempt. *Photo by Sally Lerman.*

the white sides, were the ones touching the grill. Wendy notes that the press is like a flat panini maker but without ridges. As it happens, years ago, I searched the world over for just such an appliance. I don't like ridges in my grilled cheese sandwiches. So I was very excited to attempt to re-create this original lobster roll. I picked up some lobster meat from City Fish and a bakery-fresh hot dog roll that looked bigger than standard and seemed the closest to what Wendy had described. I followed Wendy's directions precisely, and the result was different from what I had pictured. The end result looks like a long grilled sandwich. This method of heating the meat is really ideal. It's far better than the sauté method because the meat is warmed but not overcooked. The butter melts into the meat but doesn't melt enough to make the bread soggy. It really is an ingenious method. I was rather confused about the "V" concept, and I didn't really get the point of it until I actually made it. What happens is that when the sandwich is pressed, the "V" formation traps the meat so that it doesn't fall out of the edges and encases the whole thing, kind of like a Hot Pocket—very neat and tidy. Wendy said that my "V" was too shallow but noted that was more easily done with the specially made buns they used.

Wendy said most would eat it like a sandwich and that some would cut it in half, as I did. The closest comparison might be a lobster grilled cheese sandwich, but the "V" is a real innovation. I was quite surprised that I have never encountered any lobster roll even remotely close to the original. Wendy feels that this is because it was a very labor-intensive process, and most places aren't up for that today. That is too bad for us. Wendy's family retired from the business in 1976, and the restaurant closed its doors for good, making the original hot lobster roll just a memory. "Nobody makes them like that," said Wendy. "No one ever has—except us."

CHAPTER 3

Connecticut and Rhode Island

CITY FISH MARKET

884 Silas Deane Highway
Wethersfield, Connecticut 06109
860-522-3129
www.cfishct.com

City Fish is quite a family affair. The entire family works together all year long, and they appear to have a great time doing it. John Anagnos can be found here every day along with his four children: George, Michele, Davina and Telly. Mom even stopped by while I was there to pick up some of the biggest shrimp I have ever seen to include in that night's dinner. It's been this way for over eighty years since Geno Anagnos started a fish market in 1930. They came to the current location in the 1970s and started the takeout window around the same time, at first selling only fish and chips. Lobster rolls came later.

I feel very fortunate to live so close to a place that cooks and picks fresh lobster meat every day and is open year-round. There are lots of fish markets in New England, but not many get the volume of business to be able to sell fresh picked

City Fish lobster rolls. *Photo by Sally Lerman.*

lobster every day. I, for one, hate doing all the work of picking a lobster. I'm also not a fan of killing anything in my kitchen other than a bottle of wine. City Fish always has a beautiful selection of fish in its market that it sells to the public and many local restaurants. You probably wouldn't expect it on the strip mall–laden stretch of road, but City Fish also has a world-class lobster shack right in the same location. I guess "lobster shack" isn't the proper term, but it is a place where you can get lobster rolls, chowders and a variety of other shack favorites, fried and otherwise. You don't even need to take your food to go because there is a lovely, large dining area in the front, separate from the bustling fish market area, where you can relax, enjoy your hot food and have a glass of beer or wine. Telly, John's son and manager of the fish market, told me that some people just buy some lobster meat from the fish market and head in to eat it in the dining area. Genius.

The fresh picked lobster meat is what I come in here for most times. Believe it or not, even I don't always go for the full lobster roll when I'm having a lobster craving. As much as I do love lobster rolls, I also like my pants to fit. But the lobster rolls are what first brought me here and what, despite my best intentions, I usually end up buying anyway—often in addition to the lobster meat. I first came here on a tip from my boss at my day job. Perhaps she sensed my unnatural love of food, but giving me all the best tips on food when I was new to the area certainly gained her my undying loyalty.

This is, without a doubt, one of the very best lobster rolls in Connecticut for three reasons: fresh meat, bakery-fresh bread and a choice of hot with butter or cold with mayonnaise. There are other reasons, but those are the biggies. The meat is the very same fresh picked meat available in the fish market. They use meat from the tail, knuckle and claw, all cut into chunks. The hot version is heated with butter and drained so that it coats the meat but doesn't soak the bun. This one outsells the cold version eight to one—and for good reason. It allows the meat to stay tender during the heating process, and the bun is hearty enough to handle the buttery, hot lobster meat. The buns, delivered fresh from Mozzicatto's bakery, probably the most popular bakery in the Hartford area, are bigger than the average bun, and they fill it full. It is really more of a hoagie-style bun, butter grilled on the inside. The cold lobster roll is also fantastic, with the meat coated in a light amount of mayonnaise and mixed with finely minced celery. As far as I know, this is the only place in Connecticut serving freshly picked lobster meat on a bakery-fresh bun. Don't be fooled by its central Connecticut, non-scenic location—this is one of the great lobster rolls in New

England. I am very partial to a bakery-fresh bun because they are served so rarely. This is the lobster roll place I visit most frequently, but that isn't just because of its proximity to my home. I would drive well out of my way for a fix of this hearty, buttery, fresh lobster roll.

Open year-round
Hot meat with butter or cold meat with mayonnaise
Weighed in at 8.3 ounces

Captain Scott's Lobster Dock

80 Hamilton Street
New London, Connecticut 06320
860-439-1741
www.captscotts.com

When you come to the end of a little side street filled with vacant, boarded-up buildings, and your GPS tells you that you have arrived at Captain Scott's Lobster Dock, you will think it has lost its mind and might be trying to kill you. But rest assured, all is fine—just turn left when you get to the end of the street, go down an unpaved road and you will see the packed parking lot and long line of people waiting for one of the finest lobster rolls in Connecticut. Despite initial impressions, Captain Scott's is actually situated on a pleasant boat dock. On one side there is a lovely view of the boats coming and going; on the other side is the railroad. It's not as pretty, but it adds a bit of grittiness to the experience. Let's face it: docks were not always considered desirable areas

Captain Scott's lobster rolls. *Photo by Sally Lerman.*

of town, so the authentic, old-school dock experience ought to be a little rough around the edges. But the edges are the only place that's rough about Captain Scott's. The picnic tables are glossed up and exceedingly clean. The building that houses the kitchen, take-out window and ice cream stand is picture perfect. While there is no indoor seating here, most of the picnic tables are situated under a large wood-shingled pavilion, and there is even a restroom inside the building that houses the fish market. Captain Scott's actually got its start in 1993, when then lobsterman Tom Eshenfelder purchased the site with a burned-out barn, knocked it down and started Captain Scott's. Tom has since given up lobstering himself and is focused more on running the business with his sister and co-owner, Sue Tierney.

Whenever a place that sells lobster rolls is run by a lobsterman, I find that you can always count on getting a fantastic fresh picked lobster roll, and this is true of Captain Scott's. They used to cook and pick themselves, but limited kitchen space led them to start getting fresh picked meat from a local supplier. They use tail, claw and knuckle (TCK) meat here, and Tom feels that delivering a consistently great lobster roll—always tasty with the same amount of meat and topped with a pretty wedge of lemon—is what makes Captain Scott's special.

Every time I start to think that the warm lobster roll with butter just can't be done well, I have the hot lobster roll from Captain Scott's, and I'm reminded once again how great they can be. The key is how they heat up the meat. They don't sauté, which can overcook the meat. They put very small amounts of the fresh picked meat on a steam table and allow the steam to heat it up to the perfect temperature—not hot, just warm and still very tender. The meat is then placed in a grilled top-split bun, and melted butter is drizzled on top. That, in my opinion, is what makes this one work where so many others have failed. When the warm meat and warm butter combine, the butter actually sticks to the lobster meat and doesn't go straight through and make the bread soggy. Tom estimates that the hot lobster roll outsells the cold version about three to two. Both are fantastic. I can never decide which to get, so I almost always get both. And I don't regret it—that is, until I remember that I wanted to get some Maine-made Gifford's ice cream but no longer have the stomach space.

Tom also puts his own touch on the cold lobster roll. The cold, fresh picked meat is mixed with a small amount of mayo, finely minced celery, salt and pepper and put on a whole piece of lettuce, all of which is standard. The difference is that he mixes in just a bit of olive oil because he has found that it helps keep the roll together and improves the flavor. It's very innovative. I knew there must have been a secret that would make the cold roll just as good as the hot! Captain Scott's serves both small and large lobster rolls. I have never actually gotten a small. The large version of the hot and cold weighs in at about 9 ounces. Come to think of it, ordering a small version of both the hot and cold versions might give me a chance to have room for ice cream. Also, if you're sharing, I suggest you order the fry balls. I believe they are known as clam fritters, as they are chopped-up clams mixed with dough and fried. They are quite tasty here.

Open March through October
Hot meat with butter or cold meat with mayonnaise
Hot weighed in at 9.4 ounces
Cold weighed in at 8.2 ounces

SEA WELL SEAFOOD FISH MARKET

3 Liberty Street
Pawcatuck, Connecticut 06379
860-599-2082

Exactly how I stumbled across this little fish shop on the Connecticut side of the Connecticut–Rhode Island border is still a bit of a mystery even to me. I knew that many of the lobsters in Connecticut come in through the Stonington Docks area, and I decided to randomly search the Internet for lobster dealers. I saw that Sea Well had a fish shop and decided to see if it also had lobster rolls. Wow, does it ever—only the absolute best lobster roll in the state of Connecticut, and certainly among the best anywhere! Sea Well is not a new establishment; it has actually been around for thirty years. Alene Whipple's

Sea Well lobster roll. *Jane Shauck Photography.*

husband is a lobsterman who used to sell his catch to the original owner before he and Alene purchased the business seven years ago. That certainly explains why this lobster roll place is so amazing—it is lobsterman owned and lobster wharf owned.

Sea Well is actually a fun little blue shop right off Route 1, with the fish of the day written in colorful chalk across the front of the building. The shop has everything you might need for a night of seafood dining: a small amount of fresh produce, homemade soups and fish so fresh it was probably swimming in the sea yesterday. There is no seating, so you'll have to take the lobster roll elsewhere or, like me, finish it before you walk out the door.

Sea Well exterior. *Jane Shauck Photography.*

The owners at Sea Well actually have their own lobster pound at the Stonington Docks, where they buy fish and lobster directly from the fishermen and fillet everything in-house. In the store, the source of the fish is all marked, and you will find that most of it comes right from Stonington. (As it turns out, Pawcatuck is a part of Stonington.) Sea Well actually leaves the fish whole and cuts off steaks as you order them to keep it even fresher, if that's possible. As Alene says, "Only the best quality will do." That certainly applies to Sea Well's lobster roll, whose meat is picked fresh from the lobster pound every day. One thing I was really impressed with the first time I ordered this lobster roll was that they took the

Sea Well's
Shelby Smith.
*Jane Shauck
Photography*.

lobster meat directly out of the "fresh picked lobster meat" by the pound case to use in the lobster roll. There was no designated separate and lesser lobster meat used for the lobster roll. I've even seen other places that actually sell fresh picked lobster meat but use frozen meat in their lobster roll, which is just a crime.

This is really among the best lobster meat I've had; that's what really makes this lobster roll. The flavor is just incredible. It's briny and tastes, as it should, like it just came out of the sea. They take the tail, knuckle and claw meat; cut it into large chunks; and place it in a long un-grilled Martin's potato roll. Yes, you read that right: a potato roll. This is the first time I encountered this, and I have to say it was oh so right. "The hearty, sweet flavor just works," says Alene. They then top the cold meat with hot, melted butter. They also have a mayonnaise version, but I haven't tried it. Now, here's the part that is bound to be most controversial: they sprinkle chopped green onions over the top. I was skeptical myself at first, but this really works in a way I wouldn't have expected. Just let go of any preconceptions and try it once "as is"—live dangerously. I don't think you will regret it. According to Shelby Smith, actual testing went into this decision. They were looking for something to use in their lobster roll that was fresh and that they had on hand in their fresh produce section or used in their cooking already. After trying quite a few things, they found the leeks to be the unexpected winner. Not only is this one of the best, most unique lobster rolls you will find anywhere, but it happens to be one of the best deals as well. And Sea Well is open year-round. Who could ask for more?

Open year-round
Cold meat with butter or mayonnaise
Weighed in at 4.8 ounces

CHAMPLIN'S SEAFOOD

256 Great Island Road
Narragansett, Rhode Island 02882
401-783-3152
www.champlins.com

Champlin's has my favorite lobster roll in Rhode Island. One of the major reasons is because they actually use local Rhode Island lobster meat bought right from the lobstermen. This might not seem like a compelling reason. I mean, isn't it standard for a great lobster roll to use fresh, local lobster? Well, south of Maine, the answer is no. The reason is that lobster populations have been decreasing in recent years, particularly in Connecticut and Rhode Island, to the point that there really isn't much of a catch. It seems the best way to find local lobster rolls in these parts is to buy them from someone who goes directly to the source. Well, I guess not the actual source, since that would mean catching them yourself, but from the lobstermen, who can tell you where they fish.

Amanda Maybeck, the longtime manager at Champlin's, demonstrates for us the care taken in preparing the lobster meat. The lobster, mostly soft shell but sometimes hard shell, depending on the season, is cooked and picked. They then split the tail and clean it in cold water. For me, the best part was watching her chop off the big spongies before she cut the lobster meat into large chunks. As you have probably

Opposite, top: Champlin's lobster roll. *Jane Shauck Photography.*

Opposite, bottom: Champlin's. *Jane Shauck Photography.*

figured out, I'm not a fan of the spongies—the "finger" portion of the lobster claw. I find they have a strange spongy texture that can often ruin a lobster roll. Champlin's uses very finely minced celery in the lobster roll, but only during the summer, when it is in season. They find that when used in other months, it doesn't hold up well and doesn't have that good fresh crunch. I've had it both ways, and I'm not sure which I prefer. While I'm not usually a fan of celery in my lobster roll, Champlin's minces it so finely that it just seems to add an overall freshness to the roll. They serve it on iceberg lettuce and a bakery-fresh top-split bun that has been grilled. They actually use a Rhode Island bakery, Calise's bakery, for their rolls, so the whole thing is Rhode Island local. The bun is slightly larger than the standard bun, better to accommodate the generous portion of meat served in it.

For the full Rhode Island experience, Champlin's has a huge wraparound deck overlooking Narragansett Bay. They also have a lovely heated indoor seating area with wide picture windows all around, allowing you to

Champlin's. *Jane Shauck Photography.*

take in the gorgeous view. That heating part is important because they are open all year except January and February. I've gone to get my lobster roll fix in the cold months, and it really is quite a different experience from going in the summer. There are no cars and few people, and on a cold day, you can sit inside with the sun shining on you and watch the working boats go by. Oh—you can also enjoy the full-service bar in Champlin's. To continue the Rhode Island experience, I would suggest a Narragansett Summer Ale, even if it's winter. They might just have some left.

Open March through December
Hot meat with butter or cold meat with mayonnaise
Weighed in at 7.4 ounces

Chapter 4
Massachusetts

Eastwind Lobster Fish Market & Restaurant

2 Main Street
Buzzards Bay, Massachusetts 02532
508-759-1857
www.eastwindlobster.com

Getting lost can sometimes be one of the best things for lobster roll hunters. When I first found Eastwind, it was not on any of my lists, and I had never heard of it. But passing by on our attempt to find the "other" bridge onto the Cape, this place just looked so authentic and inviting that I had to stop in. It feels good to be right about a hunch—and it tastes great, too. This spot is a little Cape Cod–style shingled building by the water, right next to some boat docks that lend to the authenticity. It has inside ordering and feels like walking into a homey kitchen. Maybe that's because I'm pretty sure we had those same captain-type chairs in our dining room when I was a kid. The food takes you to the comfort of a friend's kitchen, with lots of fresh seafood and good stuff cooked from scratch. Thankfully, they are open year-round, which is a real rarity

Eastwind lobster roll. *Photo by Sally Lerman.*

in any seaside area. In the summer, you can dine outside on the large deck overlooking Buttermilk Bay while listening to some Jimmy Buffett tunes.

Craig Moore has owned Eastwind since 2004, but it was established at this location back in 1991. Experience in the seafood business makes Craig a real expert on what makes the best seafood. He buys fish, lobster and crabs daily from local fishermen for both the restaurant and fish market.

Here at Eastwind, they cook and pick the lobster meat daily, and it shows. The flavor of this meat is one that welcomes you to the Cape—fresh, tender and briny. The lobster roll is huge, overflowing with fresh, giant chunks of tail, claw and knuckle meat and weighing in at 7.6 ounces, with some whole claws on top. According to Craig, the secret to his great lobster roll is simplicity: just fresh picked meat and a touch of mayonnaise. The meat is served cold, but they will heat it on request. They do use a top-split bun here, but it isn't your standard grocery store bun; these are delivered fresh every day from George's Bakery, a local Massachusetts bakery. The buttery grilled sides on this bun are larger than usual, and the bun has a light flavor and slightly thicker density. The buttery grilled-ness is great, just like a grilled cheese.

I quickly deemed this lobster roll one of the best of the Cape, but my husband, Ken, was quick to point out that you aren't on the Cape until you cross the bridge. I now hear that point is debatable. No matter—for me, there is no debate about the fact that if you want one of the best lobster rolls on the Cape, get it before you cross the bridge.

Open year-round
Cold meat with mayonnaise
Weighed in at 7.6 ounces

CHATHAM PIER FISH MARKET

45 Barcliff Avenue
Chatham, Massachusetts 02633
508-945-3474
www.chathampierfishmarket.com

There is a sign on the wall in Chatham Pier Fish Market that says that the reason their lobsters taste better than anyone else's is because they are stored in salt water. What the

Chatham Pier lobster roll. *Photo by Sally Lerman.*

sign doesn't tell you is that the small tank you are looking at in the front of the store with the sign is far from the whole picture. That salt water isn't just any salt water. It actually comes from a sixty-foot well below the store that brings fresh, sterile seawater into not only the front tank but also the back area of the store, a huge room that houses giant tanks filled with the finest shellfish just fished from Nantucket Sound.

Chatham is one of the prettiest towns on the Cape. Provincetown is also very charming, but it's more artsy charming. Chatham is very preppy charming; in fact, it feels like the concept of "preppy" might well have originated here. Chatham Pier Fish Market is located just outside of town by the water, and at first glance, it appears to be just another lovely tourist-centric market. But it is so much more than that. It is actually a real working pier where day boat fishermen bring their daily catches to sell to Andy Baler, who runs the pier. Andy stores the lobster, crab and other sea creatures briefly in his saltwater tanks before distributing them to restaurants far and wide, including top chefs in New York City. They feel that his lobsters taste better than all others, which, in New England, is obviously saying something.

The Chatham Pier itself has been here for about fifty years, and Andy has run the pier for the last thirteen years and the market for the last six. As far as I have found, this is the only lobster pier on Cape Cod selling lobster rolls. It is a real rarity south of Maine to find this, and they aren't even that plentiful in Maine. I am always partial to lobster rolls sold by actual lobster piers because it means that they are bound to be fresher than any other. The lobster gets dropped off moments after it is caught and then it gets turned into a lobster roll only a few feet away. On Cape Cod, I've found it rather challenging, for some reason, to find lobster rolls that are fresh and use only Cape Cod lobsters. Chatham Pier's lobster roll only incorporates lobsters sourced from right off the coast of Chatham.

Andy feels that what makes his lobster roll great is the lobster meat. They cook the Chatham lobsters in a steamer every day and pick the lobsters in-house. The tail, knuckle and claw meat is served cold and mixed with a small amount of mayonnaise. I could barely contain my excitement when he told me that since I had last been there, they had changed their bun to a bakery brioche bun that they get in fresh every day. He said that his bakery distributor, LaMarca and Sons, brought in lots of samples from a variety of local bakeries before they decided on this top-split brioche bun. The bun is buttery and soft, and they grill it to crisp perfection, which, for me, really put this lobster roll into an elite category. The fresh, local meat already had it in the top tier, but to take it to the next level like this…it really doesn't get any better.

Chatham Pier's Andy Baler. *Photo by Sally Lerman.*

They are also very generous with the lobster meat here, overfilling even this somewhat larger-than-average bun. Andy says they use 5.5 ounces of meat, but I have previously weighed this one at over 10.0 ounces. You can certainly find less expensive lobster rolls on the Cape, but you'll generally get what you pay for.

Open May through October
Cold meat with mayonnaise
Weighed in at 10.7 ounces

Moby Dick's Restaurant

3225 State Highway 6 Alt
Wellfleet, Massachusetts 02667
508-349-9795
www.mobydicksrestaurant.com

Drive out Route 6 to the outer Cape in Wellfleet, near Truro, and you will find a lobster roll unlike any other and a restaurant that is entirely unique. Moby Dick's was founded in 1982 when current owner Todd Barry's parents decided to rent the former Al's Hamburgers for one season to see how it went. They then purchased it and turned it into their own place. The name "Moby Dick's" is a play on patriarch Richard Barry's nickname. The entire family has been devoted to the restaurant ever since. Todd actually met his wife, Mignon, working here. At first glance, the interior might seem like it is decorated like many other seafood restaurants with nautical paraphernalia. But upon closer inspection, you will see that each piece is unique, authentic and likely has an interesting story that Todd will be happy to share. The wood ceiling beams in the dining room came from the Wellfleet Salt Co. Todd's mother spent years collecting interesting nautical items. She had a friend who traveled to Taiwan every year to a place where old ships were dismantled and was able to score some unique items, including a real porthole with glass several inches thick. The Barrys really have a talent for displaying this eclectic collection of items in a tasteful and interesting way that invites you to come closer and see the details. The dining rooms have candles on the tables, and there is a deck area that looks out over the salt marsh.

The friendly servers—many from the British Isles, where Todd works with a program that develops young minds interested in the hospitality industry—circulate throughout the restaurant, stopping back frequently to make sure everything is great

Moby Dick's lobster roll. *Photo by Sally Lerman.*

at this merging of a full-service restaurant and takeout shack. If you order dessert, which I strongly suggest, order the key lime pie—it is life changing.

As with everything else here, Todd has put a great deal of thought into his lobster roll, and it certainly shows in the result. He has a strict policy of using only hard-shell lobsters in his lobster rolls. This is something I have rarely found in the lobster roll world, and I can't argue with the results. He thinks hard-shell lobsters have the best flavor and texture. He never uses soft-shell lobsters or "sleepers"—a term for nearly dead lobsters, which, I'm sorry to admit, are used to make some lobster rolls. When a place has many lobsters, and some start looking like they aren't moving much, restaurants need to cook them because once they are dead, they are useless. I never thought much about it, but he has a point. I imagine nearly dead lobsters are less tasty than those alive and pinching. He also feels that cooking lobsters by steaming instead of boiling is superior. He says that when cold lobsters are dropped into boiling water, it changes the temperature. Steaming, however, has a more consistent result because you always know the cooking temperature. The fresh, hard-shell, TCK meat, picked daily in-house, is mixed with a minimal amount of mayo and put on a buttery, grilled, bakery-fresh top-split bun. The bun is sourced from Calise's, a local Rhode Island bakery.

I find it inspiring when an owner puts so much care and thought into his venue and menu. It's a real find to come across a place that doesn't just try to serve decent food but also pays attention to every detail of the experience. You should most certainly plan quite a few visits to Moby Dick's during your Cape vacation.

Open May through October
Cold with mayonnaise

Moby's Lobster Bisque

2 1½-pound live lobsters
2 tablespoons olive oil
1 medium onion, chopped
1 celery stalk, chopped
1 carrot, chopped
1 medium tomato, chopped
1 head of garlic, peeled and halved
2 tablespoons fresh chopped tarragon

2 tablespoons fresh chopped thyme

8 black peppercorns

½ cup brandy

½ cup dry sherry

4 cups fish stock

½ cup tomato paste

½ cup heavy cream

1½ tablespoons cornstarch

2 tablespoons water

Fill a six-quart kettle three-quarters full with salt water and bring to a boil. Plunge lobsters into water and cook for eight minutes. Transfer lobsters to large bowl. Reserve two cups of cooking liquid. Allow lobsters to cool. Working over a bowl to catch the juices, twist off tails and claws. Reserve juices. Remove meat from tails and claws, reserving shells and body meat. (Lobster meat will not be thoroughly cooked.) Chop meat into chunks, cover and chill. In a six-quart kettle, heat oil over moderately high heat until hot (but not smoking) and sauté reserved lobster shells, stirring occasionally, for six to eight minutes. Add vegetables, garlic, herbs, peppercorns, brandy and sherry and simmer, stirring until most of the liquid is evaporated, four to six minutes. Add fish stock and reserved cooking liquid. Simmer mixture uncovered for forty-five to sixty minutes. Stir occasionally. Pour and press mixture through a fine sieve into a large saucepan. Discard solids. Stir in tomato paste and simmer until reduced, four to six minutes. Add cream and simmer four to six minutes more while continuously stirring. In a bowl, stir together cornstarch and water and whisk into lobster bisque. Add lobster meat and simmer bisque slowly over low heat until ready to serve.

WOOD'S SEAFOOD

15 Town Wharf
Plymouth, Massachusetts 02360
508-746-0261
www.woodsseafoods.com

The best dish they could present their friends with was a lobster or a piece of fish without
bread or anything but a cup of fair spring water. And the long continuance of this diet, with
their labours abroad, had something abated the freshness of their former complexion; but God
gave them health and strength in a good measure, and showed them by experience the truth
of that word, (Deut. viii.3) "That man liveth not by bread only, but by every word that
proceedeth out of the mouth of the Lord doth a man live."
—William Bradford, Of Plymouth Plantation, *1623*

It seems my Pilgrim ancestors didn't enjoy lobster nearly as much as I do. Perhaps it was the lack of bread with the lobster? That certainly could be an issue. If you're in town taking in the Pilgrim sights—the rock, the plantation, the ship and such—and you want the real Pilgrim eating experience, look no further than Wood's Seafood, right on the dock in town. There is much debate over what the Pilgrims actually ate on the first Thanksgiving, but there is no debate about the fact that they ate lobsters right out of Plymouth Harbor. Lobster might have been the Pilgrims' least favorite but most consumed protein. Wood's buys their lobsters live, directly from the fishermen who lobster in Plymouth Harbor. This is fresh, local and far more Pilgrim-authentic than pumpkin pie.

Wood's only imports lobsters from Maine and Canada in January and February, when the lobsters go into their winter dormancy from the cold harbor temperatures. Owner Jay Kimball tells us that the traps, with their delicious bait, can be right next

Wood's lobster roll. *Photo by Sally Lerman.*

to the lobster and they won't go for it. They don't move at all when the temperature here in the harbor, away from any warming Gulf Stream, gets extremely chilly. Wood's is open year-round, selling lobster and fresh seafood in their market and lobster rolls and other fantastic, simply prepared, fresh seafood dishes in the restaurant with a beautiful view of the harbor and the *Mayflower 2*, when it is in port.

Perhaps ironically, one of the three days Wood's is closed during the year is Thanksgiving Day. As Jay says, "No one wants anything but turkey on Thanksgiving." Well, strictly speaking, that's not entirely true. One year after spending Thanksgiving Day roaming about Plimouth Plantation, enjoying its full-on festivities (which I highly recommend by the way, as all the actors/residents are there in full character), we were unable to secure a seat at the always sold-out Thanksgiving dinner. So we headed into town and hit the one and only restaurant that was open, and I didn't get to have the lobster I was craving—poor me.

Wood's Seafood, in some incarnation or another, has been in this location since 1920, when it started as a fish market on the docks. The restaurant was added in 1957, and Jay believes they were selling a lobster roll from day one. If true, that would make it one of the earliest places serving lobster rolls that I have encountered.

A vintage shot of Wood's. *Photo courtesy of Wood's Seafood.*

Jay purchased it in 1989 and can be found right here most every day, making sure that only the highest quality seafood is sold and served, including on his busiest days, Christmas Eve and New Year's Eve.

The lobster roll at Wood's uses only fresh lobster meat cooked and picked at least once a day from lobsters that were purchased right out of the lobster boats. The tender tail, claw and knuckle meat is served cold on a piece of lettuce in a grilled top-split bun without anything at all mixed in. Their standard practice is to put a small amount of mayonnaise on top of the meat. This makes it quite easy to request whatever you prefer, whether it be no mayo or my choice—butter on the side for drizzling and dipping. In addition to the lobster rolls, I have actually tried quite a few of their other seafood offerings, and everything is fresh, simple and delish. Wood's is quite a find in a town where you might think that turkey would be the only game around.

Open year-round
Cold meat with mayonnaise on top

Neptune Oyster

63 Salem Street
Boston, Massachusetts 02113
617-742-3474
www.neptuneoyster.com

Neptune Oyster showed me what true hot lobster roll perfection looks like. I had heard for years that this place was amazing and had actually tried to go a few times.

Neptune lobster roll. *Photo by Sally Lerman.*

What took me so long was the wait. This is a tiny little place in the North End of Boston, the historic section where most restaurants are fairly small and the crowds are extremely large. There are only four actual tables that seat six people in the restaurant. That means that if you have a party of two, you will be seated at the same table as another party of three—very intimate. There is also a large bar with seating, and that seems to be the more ideal spot. But when you have been waiting over an hour for a seat, you take the first available. If you hadn't figured it out yet, I have a bit of a phobia about lines and crowds. I do everything humanly possible to visit popular venues when they are least crowded.

When I finally accepted that a non-crowded time doesn't exist for Neptune, I hit happy hour for some courage and then braved the crowd. While tight, the restaurant uses its space optimally. There are oysters displayed in the front window, subway-tiled walls, globe lights and marble-topped tables and a bar, giving it a retro chic speakeasy effect—perfect for a North End oyster bar.

Neptune offers both a hot-with-butter and a cold-with-mayonnaise option for its lobster rolls. I always have a hard time choosing when faced with these options. But not here—the hot lobster roll is the very best I have ever had. Achieving a perfect hot lobster roll is more of a challenge than I first realized when I started eating lobster rolls. Hot lobster rolls essentially require reheating the meat, which inevitably results in double-cooked (overcooked) meat and overly hot butter that soaks the bun so it breaks when you pick it up.

I've had hot lobster rolls done well, but never this well. Luckily, I was able to go back and speak to the chef and master of the hot lobster roll, Michael Serpa, and he shared his secrets. Although he doesn't actually consider them secrets, probably because he is clearly a top chef and unaware that he is the only chef I have encountered in my travels doing a lobster roll this way—the right way. The key, according to Michael, is not allowing the butter to separate and keeping it emulsified the whole time. The cold butter and lobster meat, sourced locally from P.J. Lobster Co. in Boston and fresh picked every day, are placed in the pan and then kept moving until the meat is warm and the butter has not separated. It sounds so simple—and he makes it look that way, as will any real pro—but it most certainly is not. I tried it at home many times without success. If your butter turns orange, you have messed up. Time to try again. Only golden, unseparated butter will do. Another reason Michael said the hot lobster roll can be more challenging to most chefs is because when lobster meat is heated, the ammonia flavor that develops if the meat isn't extremely fresh can really come out.

Michael's wife works in the kitchen with him and does the work of crafting the lobster roll. They use a generous amount of meat here. Michael says it's at least 7 ounces, but he doesn't measure it. He just wants it to look great and for people to be happy with it so they'll keep coming back for more. The warm lobster meat is spooned into a bakery-fresh long brioche bun from Iggy's in Cambridge, which was chosen by *Saveur* magazine as one of the "20 Great American Bread Bakeries." The bun is the other key to the genius of this lobster roll. It is dense enough to hold up to the melted butter without breaking. The bun is heated on the kind of grill that leaves grill lines, and it does not have flat sides.

I haven't mentioned the cold lobster roll yet, but that's not because it isn't fantastic. It's just that, in my opinion, the perfect hot lobster roll is so much more elusive. The

Neptune's Michael Serpa. *Photo by Sally Lerman.*

cold version has the same tender, briny tail, knuckle and claw meat. There is more tail meat than usual in the Neptune lobster rolls, and tail meat is my favorite. The cold meat has just a light gloss of mayonnaise, salt and pepper and is served on the same award-winning brioche.

This roll truly belongs in the elite category of the very best lobster rolls available anywhere. Meat this fresh and tasty is not easy to find, and to see it combined with not just bakery-fresh bread but award-winning, perfectly paired bread that is worthy of the lobster meat inside is very rare. If that weren't enough, Neptune blew my mind by serving up a hot buttered lobster roll unlike any other—the way it was meant to be. And although it's known as "Connecticut style," the very best one can be found in Boston.

Open year-round
Hot meat with butter or cold meat with mayonnaise

James Hook & Co.

15 Northern Avenue
Boston, Massachusetts 02110
617-423-5501
www.jameshooklobster.com

I first discovered this place when we were taking one of those bus tours around the city of Boston to get some history. We really didn't get much history at all from our guide, but we did hear all about his ex-wives, children and his stint as a nude art model. He was, however, really good for one thing: taking us to his favorite lobster

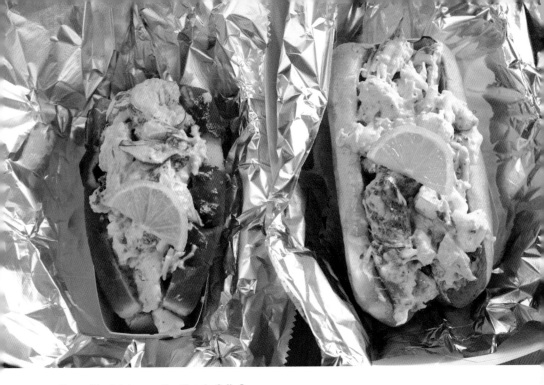

James Hook lobster rolls. *Photo by Sally Lerman.*

roll place in Boston, James Hook and Co. That made the whole tour totally worth it. And let's face it—that was what I really wanted to know about Boston.

James Hook has actually been selling lobsters from this same location since 1925, and it is still owned by the same family. There is even a James Hook still running the place! The Hooks recently experienced a fire at their retail location and are currently rebuilding and operating out of a temporary trailer. The trailer actually manages to be fairly charming with its black-and-red wood exterior and lobster paraphernalia. The retail location is situated on the water, and when you see it as you are coming over the bridge, it looks very out of place in an old-timey way. The skyscrapers rose up all around it, but the little lobster shack stayed right there, the same as it has always been. The business itself has not remained the same; it has grown into quite a lobster distributor, shipping to restaurants and lobster lovers all over the country. For those who aren't in the New England area but still feel the need for live lobster or fresh picked lobster meat, you can order online from James Hook and Co. and have it at your door the next day.

They toast the buns from Gold Medal Bakery in Fall River, Massachusetts, before filling them with the fresh picked tail, claw and knuckle meat. The lobsters

James Hook exterior. *Photo by Sally Lerman.*

are actually picked right there in the trailer, but they are boiled at their wholesale warehouse, where there is more space. They offer two sizes of lobster rolls. You might think that I would always go for the larger, but their regular size is really quite hearty, with the split-top bun overflowing with huge chunks of lobster. They are both a steal for the price, particularly considering that this is a city lobster roll. The large size is really gigantic. It comes on something like a sub roll, also fully stuffed. The meat is mixed with mayonnaise and a "secret ingredient"—very mysterious and very delicious. While the business has been here since 1925, it didn't actually start selling lobster rolls until about ten years ago for a Sail Boston event. The lobster rolls were so popular that they decided they needed to be a permanent menu item. Their lobster roll was voted "Best Boston Lobster Roll, Low-Brow" by *Boston Magazine* in 2013. There is nothing fancy about James Hook and Co. It's just fresh picked lobster rolls on the water and quality seafood the way they have been doing it for nearly ninety years.

Open year-round
Cold meat with mayonnaise

Mrs. Hook's Lobster Newburg Sauce

¼ cup flour
⅓ cup butter
1 pint hot milk
3 egg yolks, beaten
¼ cup heavy cream
Salt and a few grains of red pepper

4 tablespoons sherry
2 tablespoons brandy
1 pound fresh picked lobster meat

Using wire whisk, blend flour and butter in iron skillet over a low flame. Stir constantly while adding hot milk. Remove skillet from flame and add beaten egg yolks and cream. Return to flame long enough for eggs to cook. Season. This sauce will not separate and can be stored in refrigerator. Sherry, brandy and lobster meat are added to sauce immediately before heating in preparation for serving. Serve over toast. Makes four to six servings.

ALIVE AND KICKING LOBSTERS

269 Putnam Avenue
Cambridge, Massachusetts 02139
617-876-0451
www.aliveandkickinglobsters.com

As owner Louis Mastrangelo will be the first to point out, they don't serve a lobster roll at Alive and Kicking, they serve a lobster sandwich. And even that is a bit of an understatement. This is a marriage of lobster and bread unlike any you will find anywhere else—it's just so fantastically tasty.

Alive and Kicking, which is located in a house on a residential street in the heart of Cambridge, started selling lobsters and fish seventeen years ago, and their popularity has grown significantly since then. During the summer months, the lines are out the door for this lobster sandwich.

Alive and Kicking lobster sandwich. *Photo by Sally Lerman.*

Seeing as this isn't a particularly scenic area, and you are just a few blocks from the Charles River, you might be tempted to take your sandwich down and enjoy it by the river. But if you're anything like me, you won't be able to wait that long, and you'll gobble it down in the car before you get out of the parking lot. I'm always impressed by how good some of these city lobster rolls can be, particularly when compared to some of their country cousins. I guess when a place has a fantastic ocean view as its main attraction, it might feel like it can afford to cut some corners on the lobster roll. That's not the case in the city—the lobster roll is the one and only attraction, and it has to be worthy of hunting it down for absolutely no other reason than just how delicious it is.

The kitchen at Alive and Kicking certainly brings into question the validity of the argument that a small kitchen means you can't cook and pick your own lobsters in-house. Every day, they boil and pick fresh lobsters right here. When asked about the source of the lobsters, the saucy reply from the lobster roll craftswoman was, "The sea." Touché. I love a little sarcasm—just another benefit of the city lobster roll. In fact, the lobsters are caught mainly in Massachusetts. After cooking and picking, the TCK meat is combined with salt, pepper, mayonnaise and a "secret ingredient." Then the magic happens. They toast bakery-fresh bread from Central Bakery in Cambridge—scali-style bread, which is sliced Italian bread with sesame seeds on top—and then coat each piece with butter all the way to the edges to ensure equal butter distribution in each bite. They tell me the lobster sandwich is better unsliced, and who am I to argue with such a fantastic sandwich? The meat warms just to room temperature because of the hot bread, and the butter kind of melts into the tender, mayonnaised lobster meat, giving it the best of both worlds—butter and mayo. The bread adds interesting flavor without competing with the lobster. The size of the sliced bread makes for a perfect meat-to-bread ratio, which is often difficult to accomplish.

I really wouldn't put this lobster sandwich in any category; it is a category entirely unto itself. It's some of everything—hot, cold, mayonnaise, melted butter and whatever that secret ingredient is. Or maybe it's just the combo of everything delicious about lobster and bread coming together. They start with the basics of fresh picked lobster meat and bakery-fresh bread—a combo not easily found—and then they throw any lobster roll "rules" out the door and just go for it. This is a lobster roll that I regularly crave, and you won't find anything like it anywhere else. Luckily, Alive and Kicking is open year-round. Maybe the best thing about Cambridge isn't found on the Harvard campus after all.

Open year-round
Cold meat with mayonnaise

ROY MOORE LOBSTER CO.

39 Bearskin Neck
Rockport, Massachusetts 01966
978-546-6696

Maybe it's just because I'd never heard anything about it, but I don't know why I was so surprised to find that Rockport is a darn cute town. It's a very old-time New England seaside town with lots of adorable shops and artists' galleries, all centered on a point of land that offers stunning views of the great, wide ocean around every turn. This really is one of the prettiest New England seaside towns anywhere. It kind of reminds me of Ogunquit, Maine, a bit, but with more colonial Massachusetts in the mix.

Roy Moore's is right in the thick of the walking/shopping area. It's a cute little clapboard cottage sandwiched in the main strip of adorable little

Roy Moore's lobster rolls. *Jane Shauck Photography*.

Ken Porter of
Roy Moore's.
*Jane Shauck
Photography*.

cottages. Look for the large lobster-shaped sign that will guide you. It feels like you're just walking into a large room full of mainly lobster tanks, which you are. The main décor is an extensive collection of police patches on the wall. But this place doesn't need decoration—the house, lobster tanks and jolly characters running the show are decoration enough.

There is actually no one named Roy Moore alive or involved with the business today. Ken Porter has owned Roy Moore's for the last thirty-five years. There were three owners before him, the first of whom was Roy, who opened up a fish market at this same location in 1918. The energy in Roy Moore's is palpable, and you can't help but feel happy and in a great mood when you visit. The source of that joy and energy is, without a doubt, Ken. He clearly loves life and his work. The first time I came, I thought maybe he was just having a great day. But no—that positive energy is just radiating throughout the place every time I go. Ken's energy and excitement just can't be contained. And it's contagious, as if Santa Claus were a lobsterman bringing lobster joy to one and all.

The only cooking paraphernalia here is the soup warmer and a steamer for the lobsters. Ken carries a handful of lobsters over to the steamer like a flower bouquet. That's another great thing about this place—there's no waiting for a fresh-from-the-sea steamed lobster. They cook them all day long, and they fly out the door as fast as they can cook them. I saw quite a few men who were clearly sneaking away for a quick lobster while their wives shopped, unaware. The lobster roll is also quick. It gets pulled out of the refrigerated case and handed to you right away. I know that is bound to upset the folks who insist on their roll being buttery grilled. But I like it. This is a no-frills, no-princesses type of place.

Ken's son John has been working here all his life and clearly enjoys it every bit as much as his dad. He explains that they cook and pick the fresh lobster meat daily. They mix the lobster meat with a nearly imperceptible amount of Miracle Whip and serve it on a standard split-top bun. I admit that I'm not generally a fan of refrigerated bread, but this isn't too cold, and it tastes very fresh. It was nothing a dip in melted butter couldn't solve.

Roy Moore's. *Jane Shauck Photography.*

This lobster meat—TCK—is so good and fresh. It's torn, not chopped, and there was even visible lobster roe on the lobster meat (a real sign of freshness). I often find myself craving one of these rolls during the long winter months—or maybe I'm craving that Roy Moore's positive vibe. It's probably both.

Open March through October
Cold meat with Miracle Whip
Weighed in at 5.9 ounces

The Lobster Pool Restaurant

329 Granite Street
Rockport, Massachusetts 01966
978-546-7808
www.lobsterpoolrestaurant.com

There might not be a better place than the Lobster Pool to enjoy a lobster roll while watching a sunset over the sea. This is the East Coast after all. Lobster Pool uses this view to their full advantage. In the evenings, they have a raging fire pit set up where a contraption lets the kids roast marshmallows without getting too close to the fire. Who doesn't love s'mores? It clearly makes for a laid-back, relaxed vibe—just BYOB, kick back and take in the view. The inside of the Lobster Pool also offers glorious views from the wraparound windows, and it has kind of a rustic chic, cozy vibe going with the knotty pine walls and the old-style kettle stove for warming the place. It's a perfect spot for a fall evening.

Lobster Pool has been here since 1954. Myalisa Waring has been the owner for fourteen years, accompanied by her husband until he passed away three years ago. She has kept the business going with her children, who also work here, giving the place a real family vibe. It was challenging for her in the beginning, as her husband had always taken care of the financial side, but with help from family and friends, she figured it out because she loves the business, her employees and the customers. They clearly love her right back. It seems nobody can walk in the door without waving hello and chatting for a few minutes.

Myalisa takes great pride in the fact that she uses only fresh Massachusetts lobster, sourced from Captain Joe's and Sons in Gloucester, Massachusetts, for her lobster rolls. As well she should. Few places in Massachusetts, even

ones that use fresh lobster meat, actually use exclusively Massachusetts-sourced lobsters. I, for one, am a big fan of supporting the local fishermen. Also, when you get lobster from the local waters, it's bound to be much fresher and tastier. No matter how quickly you are able to get lobster from Maine, it's going to be longer than it takes to travel from just down the road. I know many places outside Maine take great pride in using Maine lobsters in their lobster rolls, and for places outside New England, I get it. But if there are local lobsters to be had, I would always prefer to see that. If I can see a lobster boat from where I'm sitting, I want to be eating lobster from that guy, every time.

Myalisa even keeps it local with the bread, which is sourced from George's Bakery in Medford, Massachusetts. I'm always very excited to see bread that comes from a local bakery rather than mass-produced bread. The top-split bun is grilled and then filled with the lobster meat, which is cooked and picked fresh several times a day. It's then mixed with, well, whatever you want. Unless you ask otherwise, the default is a light coating of mayonnaise. But they mix the meat to order, so you can have it how you like it—warmed with butter or without any topping at all, just ask. Lobster Pool really has a great mix of everything.

Lobster Pool lobster roll. *Jane Shauck Photography*.

Lobster Pool exterior. *Jane Shauck Photography*.

They have the view, the family love and an entirely locally sourced lobster roll. It's really worthy of a destination visit.

Open April through October
Cold meat with mayonnaise
Weighed in at 5 ounces

CHAPTER 5

New Hampshire and Maine Beaches Area

BROWN'S LOBSTER POUND

407 New Hampshire 286
Seabrook, New Hampshire 03874
603-474-3331
www.brownslobsterpound.com

Brown's and Markey's are directly across the street from each other in Seabrook. There's a reason both businesses have been here for decades. They are both high-quality seafood restaurants that are different enough to almost complement each other. Both are large, always busy, on the water and serve lobster rolls that use lobster meat that is cooked and fresh picked in-house every day. You can't go wrong with that. I recommend that you visit both (maybe on the same day) and decide which you prefer.

Hollis Brown started Brown's in 1950 in a location on Route 1 but moved to the current location for access to the saltier water that makes lobsters happiest. His son Bruce now owns the business, and grandsons Robert and Bruce run the day-to-

Brown's lobster roll. *Photo by Sally Lerman.*

day operation. And the operation goes year-round, though "only on the weekends in the winter," Robert tells me, as if that's not very much. Believe me, a longtime lobster stalker: anything open in the winter that serves fresh lobster is a find of epic proportions. I'm usually beyond thrilled to find that a place is closed only in January and February. After all, with supply and demand being what they are with lobster rolls in the winter, I might expect lobster roll places to be asking premium steakhouse prices for one of these elusive babies. Then again, I might be the only one who craves lobster rolls year-round. Brown's likes to keep it simple. The building itself is actually brown—well, maybe more of a tan, but still. It is a large wood pavilion full of picnic tables. The big difference with Brown's is that they are **BYOB**. But it's really much more than just the "B." People really pack up a whole campsite, including tablecloths, silver and glassware and all manner of accoutrements. When you plan ahead, it can really be quite fun to set up your own dining experience. But I'm not much of a planner, so I usually end up being the sad, sober one on the side eating off the standard-issue plastic plates and looking longingly at the feasters. Brown's is a great place to get a spot by one of the many huge windows, look out over the marsh and take in the wildlife. Or if you prefer, you can try to spot wildlife in the room—the ones who take the "B" part very literally and bring a bottle of booze and nothing else.

Brown's keeps their lobster roll very simple as well. They cook the New Hampshire– and Maine-sourced lobsters fresh throughout the day, cut the meat into sizeable chunks, mix it with Cain's mayonnaise and place it in a buttery grilled standard split-top bun. This roll weighed in at 4.8 ounces, with a perfect meat-to-bread ratio. They use TCK meat in the roll. Though I've always noticed quite a bit of tail meat, Robert tells me that they use less tail meat because they take the fresh picked tail meat and fry it up for their fried lobster platter. It sometimes amazes me how many lobster incarnations I have never tried. I don't tend to be much of a fried food fan, but this is fresh picked, so I might need to give it a whirl one of these days.

Open year-round
Cold meat with mayonnaise
Weighed in at 4.8 ounces

The Ice House Restaurant

112 Wentworth Road
Rye, New Hampshire 03870
603-431-3086
www.theicehouserestaurant.com

There has been an ice cream shop on this spot on Wentworth Road since the 1950s. In the summer of 1980, Keith Malinowski decided to give up working at the nuclear power plant and start a new restaurant with his wife, Kathy, that focused not just on ice cream but also the freshest seafood available. He had grown up in the restaurant business, having worked at his grandmother's place in Milwaukee, Ice House Mary's, and he decided to name his new restaurant in her honor. They now work with their daughter Meg and her husband, Drew, but you'll still find Keith in the kitchen cracking jokes and Kathy waiting tables and keeping the guests happy.

Tucked away in a wooded area, you'll see the crowds around the takeout window getting ice cream. Then look to the right and head into the restaurant. You'll find an adorable, cozy, wood-paneled dining room. The bathrooms even have murals on the walls. It might sound odd to talk about bathrooms in a food review, but it is always a good idea, in my opinion, to judge the quality of the food by the cleanliness of the bathroom. A full-on mural painted in not one but two bathrooms rightly indicates that if that much effort went into the bathrooms, the food is going to be incredible, as it is.

I generally make an assumption that if the specialty of the house is ice cream, the lobster meat is likely to be frozen. Sure, it's probably not a fair assumption, but it is pretty consistently accurate. There are only a few exceptions, Ice House being the most notable. When I first asked if the meat they used here was fresh, I learned that it was not only fresh but also came from Sanders Fish Market. Sanders happens to serve another of my favorite lobster rolls on the New Hampshire coast.

Ice House
lobster roll.
*Jane Shauck
Photography*.

Ice House's Keith Malinowski. *Jane Shauck Photography.*

I happen to think that the New Hampshire coast is one of the most underrated areas of New England. You have only about twenty miles on I-95 between Massachusetts and Maine, and I think most tend to overlook it because they're almost in Maine and probably think, "Why not go there if we've already come this far?" You will find the best and most beautiful beaches in all of New England in this area, with the only possible competition coming from the Truro and Provincetown beaches. Historic Portsmouth is one of the prettiest and most vibrant cities in New England. It's always bustling with activity and offers interesting shops and fantastic restaurants overlooking the water. But the most overlooked reason to visit the New Hampshire coast is its lobster rolls. They take a unique pride in New Hampshire in serving only the freshest local lobsters. When you ask, they will tell you exactly where a lobster came from and when it was caught—no vague answers here.

Ice House might use lobster meat from Sanders, but besides the fresh, briny flavor of the meat, they serve very different lobster rolls. Ice House uses TCK meat cut into gigantic chunks and mixed with a minimal amount of mayonnaise and a little black pepper. They then place the meat on a bed of iceberg lettuce in one of the most perfectly crisp, grilled, standard top-split buns I have had the pleasure of eating. According to Meg, "The bread should not outweigh the lobster meat." They are in no danger of having that happen with the generous amount of meat they use. I find this to be one of the most crave-worthy seasonal lobster rolls to be found on the New Hampshire coast, which is really saying something because this is a hotbed for fresh lobster rolls. This is the one that I really find myself missing during winter. I suggest you visit in October because then you'll be able to indulge in some of their homemade pumpkin ice cream, available only in the fall and certainly not to be missed.

Open April through October
Cold meat with mayonnaise
Weighed in at 7.5 ounces

Seaport Fish

57 State Road
Kittery, Maine 03904
207-475-0000
....
13 Sagamore Road
Rye, New Hampshire 03870
603-436-7286
www.seaportfish.com

I always love meeting a kindred spirit in lobster roll love, someone who takes them as seriously as I do. Jen Pettigrew told me that her mother let her try

Seaport Fish lobster roll. *Photo by Sally Lerman.*

lobster on her second birthday, thinking that a two-year-old wouldn't be into it. She grew to regret her decision to give a child such a pricey dish because it soon became Jen's favorite food, and she has enjoyed it on every birthday since. Luckily for Jen, she married a lobster purveyor, and now she can have fresh picked lobster meat whenever she wants. Seaport Fish was started in 1979 by the aunt and uncle of Jen's husband, Rich. They have been serving the freshest locally sourced fish and lobster ever since.

I had actually tried a previous incarnation of the Seaport Fish lobster roll when they used a ciabatta roll. So when Jen told me that they had decided to go with a different bun in their new restaurant, I was feeling disappointed. I am, of course, a big fan of innovative, bakery-fresh bread being used in a lobster roll. It's so rare that it happens, and I hated to hear that there would now be one fewer. Jen admitted that she really liked the ciabatta as well because it was different than everyone else's and helped set them apart. But she assured me that the new choice of bun was also great, and thankfully, they do still use lobster meat that has been fresh picked every day at their fish market. In deciding what kind of lobster roll to serve at their fish market in Portsmouth and their new restaurant in Kittery, Jen might be the harshest critic. "I'm very picky about my lobster rolls and wouldn't serve anything in our restaurant that I wouldn't serve to guests at home," she says.

Thankfully, Jen was not kidding about taking her love of the lobster roll seriously. The new version was absolutely incredible. I completely forgot about the ciabatta version. She described the new bun as a traditional New England style, but I have to disagree. This was far better than the doughy, grocery store version everyone else loves so much. This actually tastes like real, bakery-fresh goodness. Sure, it is a top-split bun, but that is where the similarities end. This bun is longer, wider and denser, and the flavor has a light sweetness. They butter and grill the sides for the perfect amount of warm crispness. Then there is the meat, which is fantastic. They use chunks of TCK meat served cold with just a glistening of mayonnaise and salt, pepper and a slight squeeze of lemon.

Seaport just opened up a really lovely restaurant in Kittery, open year-round and overlooking the Piscataqua River. The bright, open restaurant also serves beer and wine. A top-tier lobster roll with a water view and deals on the wine—it doesn't get much better than that.

Open year-round
Cold meat with mayonnaise

SANDERS FISH MARKET

367 Marcy Street
Portsmouth, New Hampshire 03801
603-436-4568
www.sandersfish.com

This fun little market, located right on the water and in the thick of the historic section of beautiful Portsmouth, has been a favorite of mine for years. I've grown to love the Portsmouth area and its beaches, and I always stop at Sanders on my way up to or back from Maine. I've usually starved myself since the departure from Hartford, and Sanders almost always serves as my breakfast—the perfect way to kick off any lobster roll binge weekend. I also love to stop by on my way home and pick up some of their spectacular fresh picked lobster meat to eat for a few days after a trip and relive the glory.

Sanders started as and remains primarily a lobster wholesaler and retailer. The business up the street, Sanders Lobster Company, has been owned by the Sanders family since 1952 and continues to be a hub for obtaining lobsters sourced from both New Hampshire and Maine. The historic, pretty blue building on Marcy Street, a gristmill in a past life, was purchased by the family in 1987 to expand their retail business. You'll always find a friendly face behind the counter, which is always filled with fresh, local fish. They also have an abundance of soups, dips and lots of other interesting dishes in the refrigerated section, along with beer and even local sodas. They also sell fresh-baked breads and a variety of fresh-baked sweets from a local baker.

This was the very first lobster roll I encountered that didn't use tail meat, and I didn't miss it. My skepticism regarding a lack of tail meat has always been linked to a suspicion about the use of previously frozen meat. Sanders immediately removed

Sanders lobster roll. *Photo by Sally Lerman.*

that suspicion, as right there in the case is fresh picked meat that appears to be primarily tail meat. Mike Sanders, who manages the fish market, explained to me that many places that serve fresh meat charge different prices for claw and knuckle meat than they do tail meat (tail meat being pricier). Sanders charges just one price for the lobster meat here, and it's usually quite a bit lower than most places.

For this lobster roll, a generous amount of cold meat is mixed with a minimal amount of mayo and then served on a unique bun, a bulky roll from Fantini Bakery in Massachusetts. This roll is similar in taste,

Mike Sanders
of Sanders
Fish Market.
*Photo by Sally
Lerman.*

texture and size to a kaiser roll. Any kind of unique roll is a real thrill for me. I love to see innovation, and this one is a great fit for lobster. What really makes the Sanders roll is the generous use of butter on the inside of the bun before grilling. It always tastes like the butter melts and drips down into the cool meat, providing a combination of both melted butter and light mayo–coated lobster meat. The meat warms up just a bit from the hot bun, and what you get is lobster-licious perfection. This is one of my very favorite lobster rolls anywhere, Maine included, and Sanders is open all year. This is the spot that I tell absolutely anyone traveling to Maine to stop by on their way, though it might set a much higher standard for lobster rolls in Maine than you might have had otherwise.

Open year-round
Cold meat with mayonnaise
Weighed in at 7.7 ounces

Jim Sanders's Baked Stuffed Lobster

Kosher salt, for water

6 live (1½ pounds each) hard–shell select lobsters, blanched

Tomalley and roe, from lobsters

1 pound cooked lobster meat, cut into small pieces

2 sleeves Ritz crackers, crushed

1 sleeve Saltine crackers, crushed

1 stick butter, melted

Lemon wedges and melted butter, for serving

Preheat the oven to 350 degrees. Bring a very large pot of salted water to a boil. Blanch the lobsters for just five minutes. Remove the lobsters, lay them on their backs and use a knife to split them down the middle—from the claws to the tail. The back shell should remain intact. Use your fingers to remove and discard the sac or "crop" behind the head. Remove and reserve in a large bowl the tomalley, roe and juices from each lobster. Place the lobsters on their backs on two rimmed baking sheets lined with foil. Gently press open the cavity to prepare for stuffing. Mix the tomalley, roe, lobster juices, cooked lobster meat, cracker crumbs and butter. Stuff the lobsters generously with the mixture. Bake about thirty minutes. Serve with lemons and melted butter.

CHAUNCEY CREEK LOBSTER PIER

16 Chauncey Creek Road
Kittery Point, Maine 03905
207-439-1030
www.chaunceycreek.com

I don't know what it is about the Chauncey Creek Lobster Pier, but I can almost feel my troubles melting away as I pull into the parking lot. Maybe there is some calming elixir in those peaceful waters and the sway of the trees. I thought it was just me, but my friend and photographer Jane also felt that way when we visited. It was like we could just sit there all day on the brightly colored, sparkling-clean picnic tables and watch the water go by. Even my husband, Ken, who has been on nearly

Chauncey Creek lobster roll. *Jane Shauck Photography.*

all my lobster roll travels, still talks about Chauncey Creek as being his favorite place. When you first arrive at Chauncey Creek, you get a feeling like you're stepping back in time to some secret riverfront hideaway. That could be because Chauncey Creek Pier has been owned by the same family, the Spinneys, since the 1920s. Ron Spinney still runs it today. In the 1950s, the family started selling lobsters and lobster rolls, and thankfully, their formula hasn't changed much since then.

One thing I've noticed about old-school lobster roll places, those venues that have been serving lobster rolls since before the 1980s, is that they don't grill the bun. Chauncey Creek doesn't have a grill, so it's not even an option. They will, however,

Chauncey Creek exterior. *Jane Shauck Photography.*

mix the lobster meat to order with whatever you want—or nothing at all—as long as they're not too busy. The reason I bring that up is because I have found among lobster roll purists that the Chauncey Creek version is somewhat controversial. Personally, I don't get why we can't accept a great deal of diversity and creativity in the lobster roll world. I mean, if every lobster roll were exactly the same, what exactly would be the point of visiting more than one place? The only essential for me is fresh picked lobster meat, which Chauncey Creek uses (theirs is also locally sourced).

This lobster roll actually uses only tail and claw meat—no knuckle involved. When I first tasted their lobster roll, I knew it was different. It was slightly sweeter and more

Chauncey
Creek's Kelly
Skanes.
Jane Shauck
Photography.

interesting in a way that really made the fresh lobster meat pop even more. I tend to appreciate the simpler, more lobster-centric flavor that results from an un-grilled white bun, and they use Country Kitchen round buns here. While very simple, the recipe they use here at Chauncey Creek is entirely different than any other I have encountered. The secret to their greatness, as manager Kelly Skanes showed us, is lightly mixing the meat with Miracle Whip, celery salt and lemon. I find that Miracle Whip instead of mayonnaise lends a sweet and pleasant flavor. However, they will make it without Miracle Whip upon request if they aren't too busy.

I'm not entirely sure why, but visiting Chauncey Creek is one of the most pleasant experiences I've had in my lobster roll adventures. Maybe it's because their lobster roll gently and enticingly encourages you to embrace lobster roll differences. Maybe it's because Kelly resembles a yoga instructor. Maybe it's the ghosts of all the happy waterside memories that have taken place over the past century. Maybe there doesn't even need to be a reason.

Open May through October
Cold meat with Miracle Whip

FOOTBRIDGE LOBSTER

108 Perkins Cove Road
Ogunquit, Maine 03907
207-251-4217

I have no idea why it took me so long to find this gem. Footbridge Lobster has been in the picturesque village of Perkins Cove in Ogunquit for the past five years.

Footbridge
lobster rolls.
*Jane Shauck
Photography.*

Perhaps that's part of the reason, as Perkins Cove is nearly inaccessible by car in the summer months. It's also always completely packed, with a line stretching down the road (and I might have mentioned that I have a bit of an aversion to crowds). But Perkins Cove is packed for good reason. It boasts an adorable collection of shops with artisan-crafted items and restaurants full of tasty, unique foods. And if that weren't enough, it's situated right on the ocean and has a cliff walk that goes around the cove, with lots of benches for taking in the view. There is actually a secret to visiting Perkins Cove: go early. Many of the shops and restaurants open on Easter weekend, before the hordes of people have arrived. And let's face it—a trip to Maine isn't about taking a dip in the icy water anyway, even in the summer.

Opening day of Easter weekend is when I first sampled this fantastic lobster roll. It has absolutely everything I look for in a lobster roll. First, the location is owned by a lobsterman, Chris Eager, so the roll is packed full of the absolute freshest lobster you can find, probably swimming yesterday. Lobstermen never serve frozen meat in a lobster roll; they know what a crime against lobsterdom that would be. The lobster meat is picked at their processing area on Badger Island in Kittery every day and delivered directly from there to your lobster roll in Perkins Cove.

This is lobster meat the way it should be—minimally messed with and barely cut. You get tons of huge chunks of tail and claw meat, with most of the spongies trimmed off (just one or two for color). The lobster meat is mixed to order, so you can have it with either butter or mayonnaise. I don't know which I would recommend because both are delish. I guess it just depends what kind of mood you're in. The lobster meat is then placed in what I consider the holy grail of lobster roll searching: a bakery-fresh bun. The bun should satisfy any bun purists out there, as it is a top-split, white bread bun. It's also baked fresh and delivered every day, which means it has far more flavor than a grocery store bun and none of the stuff to make it shelf stable and less delicious. They butter and grill the bun and then overstuff it with that fresh meat. Chris says they use 5.0 ounces of meat, but I weighed it in at 6.7 ounces—and that's barely cut meat, so there isn't much surface area for mayo to weigh it down.

Footbridge is an adorable wood-shingled food stand overlooking the water. Forget about seating—you don't need it anyway. Save the two chairs situated in front for someone else. Take your lobster roll out to the ocean walk and claim one of those benches overlooking the sea. It doesn't get much better than that.

Chris is not just a lobsterman who owns a lobster roll stand; he is truly a passionate prophet of the sea-to-table philosophy. While you are waiting for your order, check out the television. It has a live feed directly from the *Miss Mae* so that you can watch Chris and Tristin Boyd, his deck hand, work daily to haul in their eight hundred lobster traps in rotation. Chris

Footbridge's Chris Eager. *Jane Shauck Photography*.

was generous enough to take Jane Shauck and I out on the *Miss Mae* to fully experience where a lobster roll starts. And it starts early—I can tell you that. They were nice enough to push back their 4:00 a.m. start time thirty minutes for us. That's right, Chris and Tristin load up the *Miss Mae* every day and head out of Badger's

Footbridge's
Tristin Boyd
on *Miss Mae*.
*Jane Shauck
Photography*.

Island at 4:00 a.m. to catch lobster in spring, summer and fall. And in the winter, when lobsters go dormant, they harvest scallops. Footbridge Lobster, however, is open only from Easter to Columbus Day.

Chris and his wife started Footbridge Lobster in 2008, and it has turned into a family business. Family members work the stand and can tell you all about the *Miss Mae*, Chris and the relatively short trip that was made from the sea to the lobster roll in your hand. This is why I am extremely partial to lobster rolls from lobsterman-owned establishments, of which there are very few. No one is going to look at you like you have six heads when you ask where the lobster was sourced or if it was previously frozen. They will smile, point to the television screen and show you that there is no middleman here, no long transport and storage. It's just fresh lobster from the man who caught it served on a local bakery-fresh bun at a place by the ocean.

Open April through October
Cold with mayonnaise or butter
Weighed in at 6.7 ounces

THE CLAM SHACK

2 Western Avenue
Kennebunk, Maine 04043
207-967-3321
www.theclamshack.net

The Clam Shack's lobster roll is the lobster roll to which all others are compared and found wanting. If I get to choose my one last meal on this earth, this lobster roll

Clam Shack lobster roll. *Jane Shauck Photography*.

would be it—combined with my mother's lemon meringue pie, which is the perfect complement to lobster rolls, by the way. It certainly isn't for lack of trying that I have yet to eat a lobster roll that is superior to the Clam Shack's. Recently, I have tried a few that came close, and I even wondered if I was just holding some sentimental attachment to the Clam Shack lobster roll. So, every time I find a contender, I stop by the Clam Shack within a day or so, and sure enough, no matter how many times I try it, it is even better than I remember. This lobster roll accomplishes its greatness with a combination of all of the elements. The meat, bread and butter are superior to most every other lobster roll, but when tried individually, I could not say that there is any one component that really makes it. The magic happens when it all combines in your mouth at just the right temperature. I suppose maybe it's like French food or other fine cuisine—you have to get every element in every bite or you aren't experiencing it correctly.

Believe it or not, the Clam Shack lobster roll was actually the very first lobster roll I ever tried. I had enjoyed lobster many times growing up because it was my grandmother's—an eleventh-generation New Englander—very favorite food. But it wasn't until my brother John and I were driving up to visit her sister, Aunt Gladys, in Maine and stopped off in Kennebunkport for some lunch that I had my first lobster roll. There I saw it on the menu: fresh picked lobster meat on a bun with butter or mayonnaise or both. That moment changed my life forever. It was literally the greatest thing I had ever tasted in my life. It also ruined me forever because I then thought that every lobster roll would be as good as the Clam Shack's. That is really when Lobster Gal was born and I started my wild obsession with traveling all over New England in search of truly great lobster rolls. The next few lobster rolls I tried after my first were not great, but they weren't any less expensive, and the exterior didn't look any less authentic. I realized that the only way to know for sure was for someone to eat and document every lobster roll and to share that knowledge so that the scam of trying to pass off lesser lobster rolls for high prices to unsuspecting tourists would end. And so my life's work began. Just think about it—if the first lobster roll I tried had been "meh" or bad, I might never have given them another shot and never would have gained this wealth of lobster roll knowledge.

When I actually met and had a chance to sit down and talk with Steve Kingston, owner of the Clam Shack and the man behind the legend, it was lobster roll kinship from the start. Never before have I met someone who takes lobster rolls as seriously and thinks about them nearly as much as I do. He is constantly thinking of ways to make his already flawless lobster roll even better. He shared that on his first visit to the Lobster Roll Rumble in New York City, a faceoff of the most elite lobster

Clam Shack food prep. *Jane Shauck Photography*.

rolls, he decided to change his butter brand to Kate's to make his lobster roll entirely Maine made. He was thoroughly impressed with the result and made the change permanent. By the way, Clam Shack has won the competition in both of the years that they participated. I went to the Rumble for their first year, and I knew they had the best lobster roll in the room. I had tried nearly all of them before, but I was impressed with how quickly the crowd figured it out, too. No other table in the room had a line any longer than five or so people. All night long, the line for the Clam Shack lobster roll stretched across the room and had probably one hundred people. Clam Shack won indeed, but I feel the magnitude with which they blew everyone else out of the water is lost in articles about the evening.

The greatness of the Clam Shack lobster roll really starts in the freshness of the lobsters. These lobsters are caught within twenty-four hours of being served up on a bun. We had a chance to take the boat out into Cape Porpoise Harbor and stand

Cooking at the Clam Shack. *Jane Shauck Photography.*

on the dock with Eric Emmons, a fifth-generation Maine lobsterman, and watch the lobstermen bring in their catch. It really is something to see. All of the crates of lobsters come in and are stored underneath the small wooden floating pier. After an afternoon of taking in the catch, Eric brings the lobsters back to land and drives them a few miles up the road to the Clam Shack, where they are stored in the large tanks full of circulating salt water being pumped up from the tidal river below. Steve regularly tests the salinity, pumping the water in at peak saltiness when the tide is coming in.

Clam Shack's
Steve Kingston.
*Jane Shauck
Photography.*

Bright and early the next morning, Mike Cymbrak, or "the MotherShucker," as he is affectionately known, will start the work of cooking the lobsters—fifty at a time—by boiling them in fresh seawater, also pumped in, over a wood-fired stove. Then Mike gets to work shucking so fast you can barely see his hands move; this is a master at work. They even clean the meat in salt water. It's a system that makes an OCD girl smile. The meat is neatly sorted into split tails, whole claws and knuckles. It is then portioned into cups so that each includes at least two luxuriously curled half tails, two whole claws and some knuckle meat. The meat is then stored on ice because Steve believes that keeps it at exactly thirty-two degrees, the ideal temperature for the short-term storage between being picked and served that same day.

They use only soft-shell lobster meat because they believe the meat is sweeter and more tender, as do most lobstermen in Maine. Steve feels that each part of the lobster—the tail, claw and knuckle—imparts a different flavor and has a different texture and that for the full lobster roll experience, a little bit of each should be in every bite. Don't be afraid that the large, uncut tail meat curls or whole claws will be pulled out of the bun with your first bite, as can happen with tougher meat. This meat is perfectly tender, and your teeth will cut through a perfect bite without any effort. And although I knew the answer already, I asked anyway because I ask every owner: "Do you ever use previously frozen meat in your lobster roll?" I quite liked Steve's answer: "Sacrilege! No frozen meat for any reason ever!"

Then, as the busloads of people start arriving, Steve and his crew get to work in the compact prep area crafting the perfect lobster roll. The other key, which I tend to think is the real secret, is the bun they use here, which is delivered fresh from Reilly's Bakery in Biddleford, Maine. As Steve says, "The fresh yeast roll perfectly complements the salty sweet lobster." It's a round bun, very light with a soft texture. The flavor is difficult to describe. It's white bread, but it has far more flavor than any standard bun. You can't just go purchase this bun either; it is made specifically for the Clam Shack. That's what I think sets this lobster roll apart from every other lobster roll in Maine. You can't get anything remotely similar anywhere else, and you can't make it yourself. It can only be experienced as it should be—right there in Kennebunkport.

I always go with the butter-only option here, with additional melted butter for dipping. What can I say? I really like butter a lot. Don't forget to squeeze the lemon wedge on the lobster meat for optimal perfection. Steve prefers both butter and mayonnaise on his lobster roll. For assembly, they grill the bun on the inside to crisp buttery perfection and then immediately add the cool lobster meat. Next, they drizzle melted butter on the meat and/or spread mayonnaise on the top of the bun and then close it and call your number. Ignore any temptation to take your lobster roll elsewhere to enjoy it. Eat it right when it makes it to your hand, when all the components are at their optimal temperature. Just look around and grab the nearest seat available—you won't be thinking about anything other than the perfection in your mouth, anyway. When I'm fully planning my experience (usually my third one of the day), I will buy a fresh-squeezed lemonade if they have the stand set up and claim a spot on a bench alongside the building, overlooking the river and the town.

Steve is such a presence here that it's easy to think he has always owned the Clam Shack, but it actually opened in 1968 as a takeout stand next to a classic seafood market called Shackford & Gooch, which had been here since 1938. The Clam Shack's owner at that time, Richard Jacques, ultimately bought the fish market in the '70s, combining the two businesses. Steve bought the property in 2000 and, as he puts it, "makes fresh product, great service and award-winning food the priority." Any changes to the building have been made with historic preservation in mind.

"Fresh. Period. We buy direct and do all our own cooking, shucking and cleaning. Our lobster meat is truly sea-to-table within the same day—never frozen, never compromised." That's what Steve says makes his lobster roll great. But if you ask me, there is so much more than that. I really did not think it was possible to like this lobster roll any more than I already did (I already like it more than lots of people in my life). But there are few food items that you can watch being made from the

Clam Shack lobster meat. *Jane Shauck Photography*.

beginning to end and actually like them better. This is, after all, food, and it's not always a pretty process. But to talk to Steve and actually experience and see how much thought and care goes into each and every step was impressive. Every single step is tested, thought through and executed with precision to craft the lobster roll that is true perfection.

Open May through October
Cold meat with mayonnaise, butter or both
Weighed in at 6.5 ounces

The Clam Shack Lobster Roll

FOR FOUR PERFECT LOBSTER ROLLS, YOU'LL NEED:

Four one-pound lobsters (we boil ours in salt water for fifteen minutes)
Melted butter
Your favorite white bread rolls (a hot dog bun is traditional, but we use a handmade bakery roll)
Mayonnaise of your choice

Crack and pick the lobster tail, knuckles and claws. Melt a bit of butter in a skillet and grill the rolls, cut side down, until golden. Smear on a bit of mayo and pile the meat on the buns. Drizzle melted butter over the lobster and serve with a lemon slice. That's the taste of Maine!

OLD SALT'S PANTRY

5 Ocean Avenue
Kennebunkport, Maine 04046
207-967-4966

No day in Kennebunkport is complete without some time spent wandering through town and poking around the many unique little shops. Right in the center of town, you'll find a little building with window boxes spilling over with flowers called Old Salt's Pantry. You wouldn't necessarily know at first glance that a truly great lobster roll is to be found there. The shop sells assorted Maine-centric items such as maple syrup and Maine blueberry jam. Old Salt's, which was established in 1984, is a delicatessen with a very

Old Salt's lobster roll. *Jane Shauck Photography*.

creative menu and what appears to be quite a following among locals. Especially popular are their breakfast sandwiches, which are more like breakfast hoagies.

Behind the counter, you'll find the pleasant, youthful owner, John Belyea, far from the "Old Salt" indicated on the sign. Watching John work was like watching a master craftsman. He doesn't just cook and assemble the sandwiches; he works with great care to create masterpieces. And that's not just for the lobster roll—watching him make an egg sub was equally as impressive. He takes sandwiches very seriously, making sure to select the freshest and best ingredients, cook them to order and then make them beautiful. "Everything at Old Salt's is made to order...nothing is pre-portioned. I make each roll until I'm satisfied it's going to be great!" says John.

Space in Old Salt's kitchen is very limited, but John makes the most of it. He gets his lobster meat cooked and picked fresh every day from the fabulous Port Lobster, right down

Old Salt's John Belyea. *Jane Shauck Photography*.

the street. There is no set amount of meat in his lobster rolls, but it's always a hearty portion. He simply adds enough tail, claw and knuckle meat until it looks perfect. Even his philosophy about how the lobster meat should be prepared is executed with precision. He never chops the meat, preferring instead to tear it by hand, and he never mixes it with anything. That's right—it's just chilled, naked lobster meat placed on finely chopped, crisp lettuce and served on a bun with a thin coat of mayonnaise. It also comes with a side of hot butter and a lemon—this guy thinks of everything. He has no specific brand loyalty for his bun—it's just a standard top-split New England bun, buttered and grilled on the sides. The result of the fresh meat, minimal topping, lettuce and lemon is unusually bright and refreshing. I don't normally care for lettuce on my lobster roll and almost always pick it off and pretend it never existed, but I actually enjoy it on this one. Some lobster rolls can tend to feel quite heavy and sit in your stomach like a rock for hours. John's roll leaves you feeling like you just ate the fresh, low-fat, healthful protein that lobster actually is. Well, unless you use up that whole side of butter.

Open April through December
Cold meat with mayonnaise

CHAPTER 6

Midcoast Maine

EVENTIDE OYSTER CO.

86 Middle Street
Portland, Maine 04101
207-774-8538
www.eventideoysterco.com

Eventide's is easily the most chic lobster roll to be had in Maine. I'm not saying that there is stiff competition, as Maine isn't really known for its chicness, but still, this restaurant could go head to head with the best of New York. I suppose I expected something different, having judged it by its fine food pedigree and awards. I expected that I would need to budget time for a fancy sit-down dinner, but I was pleasantly surprised to find that it is actually more of a high-end, casual chic bar/eatery. In addition to several tables, there is a bar with a huge block of Maine granite holding an assortment of beautifully displayed oysters from Maine and beyond. Another bar seating area lines the large window facing the sidewalk and is perfect for drinking and people-watching. I'm very into their concept, which

Eventide
lobster rolls.
*Photo by Sally
Lerman.*

seems designed for people who want to drink and have small plates of finely crafted food without having to go through the whole process of a fill-yourself-to-the-brim multicourse meal. The young, beautiful, foodie hipster vibe is topped off with just the right amount of retro chic, exemplified by the gentleman behind the bar sporting a waxed handlebar mustache.

The real source of the retro-inspired foodie vibe is the owner, Arlin Smith. For Arlin, the whole idea behind Eventide Oyster Co. was to revive a very old concept: the oyster bar. To execute the concept, he didn't just use his skill in creating gourmet food; he really studied the history of the food items and venues. In creating his old-style chowder, he researched and thought about what fishermen sitting around the campfire might have had on hand for cooking. He's about creating food as it was traditionally served and originally conceived. Arlin isn't re-creating the originals; he's more of the school of thought that you need to know the rules in order to break them and create something truly unique.

There can be no debate that Eventide Oyster Co.'s lobster roll selections are uniquely their own. The warm version is a brown butter vinaigrette lobster roll that will change your life. It is a bit sweet but also light, as the brown butter coats and covers the meat without soaking into the bun. This might not sound like a big deal, but I have never seen a warm lobster roll executed in such a way. This must be what happens when a world-class chef takes on the lobster roll. Arlin does things that seem impossible in the world outside Eventide Oyster Co. I'm sure there are other genius ingredients in the brown butter lobster meat, but I don't know what they are—and I don't need to. Some things just shouldn't be attempted at home. One thing that I didn't notice was vinegar, which I expected due to the name. I'm not sure if it's just an honorary name or if there is just such a slight amount of vinegar that you can't taste it. Perhaps he simply transformed the ingredient so that it is indistinguishable. It tastes in no way like a salad vinaigrette.

For their bun, Eventide most daringly chose to break the lobster roll rules with an Asian-style bun that is made in-house and steamed to order. When I first encountered this bun, I thought that it was all wrong. It was too light and too sticky, and it was never going to stand up to lobster meat. I also thought that it looked very small, giving the lobster roll the appearance of a slider instead of a full-size meal. How wrong I was. This bun, like everything else here, was brilliant. The bun actually melts into each bite and adds just a bit of flavor while allowing the lobster meat to shine. It is every bit as tender as the lobster meat inside. Despite initial appearances, this lobster roll weighs in at just over 5 ounces, which is on par with the weight of most average-sized lobster rolls.

As for the meat, I have saved the best for last. This is really what makes this lobster roll incredible, and no, you have never had lobster meat quite like this. Arlin cooks the meat in a way that is entirely his own. After the local Maine lobster is killed, it's cooked in a combination moist- and dry-heat oven and then picked and pulled by hand into small pieces. The result is meat that is the most tender I have ever had. It has an incredible flavor and texture, as the tail meat is as tender as the steamed bun.

In addition to the brown butter lobster roll, there is also a cold lobster roll with sea salt, lemon, mayonnaise and a bit of dill. Arlin's favorite is the warm version, but I could not decide which I liked best. I would suggest trying both. They also have a hollandaise version, which I have yet to try. As with most genius, we might never truly understand the Eventide Co. lobster roll—and we weren't meant to. Let go of your conceptions about what a lobster roll should be and just enjoy it. Take a Saturday, find a nice people-watching spot at the bar and enjoy the fruits of culinary genius. Eventide is open year round, so go there now.

Open year-round
Cold with mayonnaise or hot with butter
Weighed in at 5.1 ounces

FISHERMEN'S GRILL

849 Forest Street
Portland, Maine 04103
207-699-5657
www.fishermensgrill.com

When asked what makes his building great, Mike Nappi is not afraid to tell you: "Not much; we joke about how crappy it is." I have to love that kind of honesty, particularly because once you join the group of in-the-know lobster roll lovers who have had this masterpiece, you won't even notice the venue. Mike, a former personal chef, bought Fishermen's Grill from the previous owner in early 2013 and has been working to put his own twist on the place while sticking to the concept of super-fresh lobster rolls that has had this little hole in the wall quietly gaining quite a reputation in the past few years. In the summer, the line can stretch well around the building for most of the day. Once you go here, you'll realize that its popularity is not at all related to its proximity to any well-traveled tourist route. You'll need your GPS to find it, and even with that, you'll need to slow down to look for the tiny shack tucked back between a seafood market and a Chinese restaurant. On a busy day, you won't be able to find a seat. Mike is thinking of adding a takeout window, but he refuses to speed things up or "go production" if it means sacrificing any aspect of what makes the food great.

According to Mike, who hails from Philly, the key is using the highest-quality seafood. I guess that explains their tagline: "Seafood so fresh, you'll wanna slap it!" Getting the best seafood on a consistent basis isn't as easy as you might think, even in Maine. But Mike is committed to quality. He inspects each delivery personally and sends it back if it's not up to snuff, even if that means a popular item not making it onto the menu that day. Fishermen's Grill is open year-round, and Mike thinks

Fishermen's Grill lobster rolls. *Photo by Sally Lerman.*

that really speaks to the quality of the food. The customer base isn't just made up of tourists who are coming one time; Fishermen's Grill has a devoted local fan base that keeps coming back for more.

"The love," according to Mike, is what makes his lobster roll great—both his love of food and the love that he puts into making it. I must say, the love really shows in his lobster roll. In the winter, the rolls are cooked to order, meaning that you order a lobster roll while the lobster is still alive. It takes a bit longer, but it's so worth the wait. During summer, he gets in early in the morning to cook and shuck the lobsters. His lobster roll is about 75 percent tail meat, partly because he uses culls (one-clawed lobsters) but also because he feels that so many places use frozen claw and knuckle meat, and he really wants to make it clear that his lobster roll is different. This is real, fresh meat—never frozen or prepackaged. He mixes the huge chunks of tail meat and whole claws lightly with mayo, sea salt and freshly ground pepper and puts the meat in a buttery grilled top-split bun that he gets fresh from a local bakery. When the commitment to freshness extends not just to the lobster meat but also to the bun and even the pepper, the result is pure lobster roll perfection.

Mike serves three sizes of lobster rolls: mini (4.5 ounces), classic (6.5 ounces) and jumbo (9.5 ounces), all on the same size bun and packed full of meat. He was even quite modest when I pulled out my scale to test the claim that there were 9.0 ounces of lobster meat and found that it actually weighed in at 11.0 ounces. He says, "Well, the bun and the mayo weigh something." That's true, but that's how I compare the weight of lobster

Mike Nappi of Fishermen's Grill with The Franklin.
Photo by Sally Lerman.

rolls since I can't weigh them prior to assembly, and the jumbo is certainly one of the more generous I've seen.

After I had seen what I thought were some generous lobster rolls, Mike decided to reveal his latest creation. The Franklin is three full pounds of meat piled into a foot-long bun and shaped into a veritable mountain of a lobster roll. Never before have I laid eyes on anything more beautiful. It was just breathtaking. I haven't personally attempted to conquer this behemoth…yet. But if you're feeling adventurous, they have a food challenge involving The Franklin and other sides that has yet to be mastered. It truly is the king of all lobster rolls.

Open year-round
Cold with mayonnaise or hot with butter
Jumbo weighed in at 11 ounces

Bite into Maine

Fort Williams State Park
1000 Shore Road
Cape Elizabeth, Maine 04107
207-420-0294
www.biteintomaine.com

The first time I visited the cute silver purveyor of tastiness that is the Bite into Maine trailer, I had quite a bit of trouble finding it, which resulted in a fair amount of mockery. Apparently, I'm the only person on earth who wasn't aware that Fort Williams Park, home to the Portland Head Lighthouse, is one of the most

Bite into
Maine
lobster roll.
*Jane Shauck
Photography.*

famous spots in Maine. Hey, what can I say? I don't go to Maine to hunt lighthouses; I go to hunt lobster rolls. And I caught a real prize with this one. As it happens, Portland Head Lighthouse really is one of the prettiest spots in Maine. Thank goodness they have this lobster roll there or I might have never seen this picturesque lighthouse on a hill overlooking the ocean. I actually think one of the best parts about being lobster roll obsessed is that I end up finding some of the most beautiful off-the-beaten-path spots that I never would have encountered had I not been on the hunt.

Bite into Maine has renewed my faith in the food truck. If you've poked your head into a few food trucks, you know that they're not known for their cleanliness. Bite into Maine's interior, however, is truly spotless and sanitized—the stainless steel just gleams! Anyone who takes that much pride in cleanliness is bound to take even more pride in their actual food. Karl and Sarah Sutton are really some of the nicest people I've had the pleasure of meeting on the lobster trail, and they seem to be a great team. Of course, they need to be being in such close quarters all day.

Karl and Sarah moved to Maine from Minnesota in 2004 and started thinking about the food truck concept.

Bite into Maine exterior. *Jane Shauck Photography*.

They wanted to choose one food item and do it very well. The Suttons quickly found that nobody was putting a creative twist on the traditional Maine- or Connecticut-style lobster rolls. In New England, that's because most lobster roll lovers are extreme purists, Puritans even! They wouldn't dream of messing with tradition, and if you do, you're off in crazy world. Thank goodness for some outside perspective.

Bite into Maine offers five lobster roll options: "Maine," cold and tossed with butter; "Connecticut," cold and served with melted Cabot butter on the side

Bite into Maine's Sarah and Karl Sutton. *Jane Shauck Photography*.

(Although, technically speaking, this is not actually Connecticut style since the meat would need to be warm and tossed with butter. There I go again being a purist!); "Picnic," with coleslaw on the lobster roll; the spicy "Chipotle" version; and "Wasabi," which sounds crazy but is unexpectedly delicious. They use fresh cooked and picked claw and knuckle meat from a local supplier, as their prep space is quite limited. That makes the Bite into Maine lobster roll one of only two among my favorites that don't use tail meat (the other is Sanders Fish Market in Portsmouth, New Hampshire). Recently, they started using a bakery-fresh bun, and I almost couldn't contain my excitement. So few places use a bakery-fresh bun, and when a lobster roll I already love takes it to that next level, my joy can't even be expressed. The local baker, who is very talented, wishes to remain nameless. Who doesn't love a little lobster intrigue?

Sarah always wanted to be a food stylist, and it certainly shows in the beautiful lobster rolls she presents. The 2013 season was only their third, and they are now gaining well-deserved popularity far and wide. They were one of only three Maine establishments (along with Clam Shack and Eventide Oyster Co.) invited to join the Lobster Roll Rumble in New York City in 2013. This year was their first winter season at Sunday River. I, for one, am thrilled that this lobster roll will be available year-round, even if it means I have to take up skiing.

Open in Fort Williams Park May through October
Open at Sunday River Ski Resort December through April
Cold meat with mayonnaise, butter or other options
Weighed in at 7 ounces

Gurnet Trading Co.

602 Gurnet Road
Brunswick, Maine 04011
207-729-7300
www.gurnettrading.com

When you see Gurnet Trading Co. pop up on the side of the road, it comes as a bit of a surprise. It's just a short drive outside the hustle and bustle of Brunswick. I should mention that no trip to Brunswick is complete without a trip to Gelato Fiasco for the finest gelato on earth. The burnt sugar gelato (they call it something else I can never remember) is life changing, and the mango is the perfect antidote if you feel a lobster roll overdose coming on.

Right outside town is an adorable little shack on the side of the road all decked out with lobster paraphernalia. It looks like it should be next to the ocean instead of right next to the road, but there is a lovely view of the river if you step down to the lower seating area. I always wondered about the location until I had a chance to speak to the owner, Julia Soper. As it turns out, the spot was actually a junkyard until the Sopers purchased it ten years ago and turned it into a seafood mecca. Inside, you'll find a cozy little fish shop with a lobster tank and the menu written out on the chalkboard. It's very charming in that old-school way. They recently added a little seating area, and although it's small, it's pleasant and perfect for a place that is open year-round. As Julia's daughter Sarah says, "We aren't just a seasonal tourist shack…the locals love us and are regulars in the store year-round."

People know fresh, quality seafood when they find it, and the Sopers were in the seafood business for quite some time before they started Gurnet. Julia's husband has actually been diving for scallops and oysters for thirty years. He started off selling

Gurnet's lobster roll. *Photo by Sally Lerman.*

his scallops door to door, and they now have fifteen lobster boats and a wholesale wharf in Cundy's Harbor.

The lobster roll at Gurnet is made with freshly caught, never frozen lobsters that are cooked and picked in-house every day. They use large chunks of tail, claw and knuckle meat and a bit more mayonnaise than I generally prefer. But they do make the lobster rolls to order, so you can get it with "clear meat," as they and some others I've seen call lobster meat without anything on it. I, however, prefer to call it "naked." You can also request your lobster meat with butter if you prefer. Julia prefers to use only white pepper in her lobster rolls; she is not a fan of black pepper in anything. The meat is then placed in a standard split-top bun that has been buttered and grilled on both sides. The result is pure delight.

Gurnet is really quite a find because it is not far off the beaten path yet has all the charm of a place that is. It also offers a water view and is owned by a lobster wholesaler, ensuring freshness. Best of all, Gurnet is open year-round. It is a true rarity to find a place in Maine serving a fresh picked lobster roll in the winter, especially one this good.

Open year-round
Cold meat with mayonnaise
Weighed in at 6.5 ounces

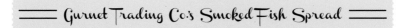

Gurnet Trading Co.'s Smoked Fish Spread

4 ounces smoked salmon
4 ounces smoked whitefish
16 ounces cream cheese softened
¼ cup finely chopped dill pickles
¼ cup finely chopped Vidalia onion
Dash of dill
Dash of white pepper

Mix all ingredients together and serve with crackers.

Erica's Seafood

6 Malcolm Drive
Harpswell, Maine 04079
207-833-7354
www.ericasseafood.com

As it turns out, Erica is not the head chef at Erica's; she is the owner's twelve-year-old daughter. I say "chef" because when I first tried this lobster roll, I assumed it was run by a chef—it's just that good. Erica's is a fairly new establishment. Tom and Andrea Hunter built the wharf in 2003. In case you don't know, a wharf is not, as I had always assumed, a pretty place on the water where people bring boats. A lobster wharf is actually a working dock designed as a place for lobstermen to bring their catch and sell it to the wharf, which then distributes it from there. Lobstermen almost exclusively sell their lobster catch to a wharf. So when a lobster wharf decides to open a stand to sell lobster rolls, it is a particularly joyous occasion for lobster lovers because it means that we will actually have the opportunity to eat lobster that might have been swimming wild and free in the sea that morning. It doesn't get much fresher for those of us who aren't actually out there catching them.

After Tom and Andrea had the wharf going for a few years, they started selling retail lobsters in 2009 and opened the cutest stand you have ever seen in 2011. I use the word "stand" instead of "shack" because something this adorable and colorfully and tastefully decorated could never be mistaken for a shack. The purpose and result, of course, is the same, but it just makes me smile to see something like the dollhouse/playhouse I wished I had as a kid with pretty red picnic tables serving my favorite food, perfectly executed. I suspect Erica might have a hand in the décor at Erica's—it's a girl's dream. As if that weren't enough ambience, there is the gorgeous view of Casco Bay and, my personal favorite, a canine greeter. Out here at the remote end of Harpswell Point, dogs just roam

Erica's lobster roll. *Photo by Sally Lerman.*

about enjoying the scenery. Have no fear—these are smart dogs. They know to stay away from moving cars, and it's rather impossible to drive too fast on the unpaved streets. As you get out of your car, Brandy, the tan "American Classic" (my preferred name for mixed-breed dogs), greets you and then goes back to her business of following around her beloved dad, Tom.

I actually stumbled upon Erica's the first time I came to Harpswell Point in search of lobster rolls. I had never heard of it, it wasn't on my list and I couldn't find a thing about it online. But its wharf-side location, charming exterior and sign advertising two lobster rolls for twenty dollars beckoned. While I normally assume very inexpensive lobster rolls use previously frozen meat, the authentic look of this place suggested otherwise. This really is one of my best finds to date. Andrea gets fresh cooked and picked lobster meat from her husband every morning, straight from the boats that fish in the bay. The tail, claw and knuckle meat is cooked to perfection, leaving it tender and briny, as it should be. Considering the price, you might expect less meat. This lobster roll is piled into a buttery grilled traditional Country Kitchen bun and weighs in at 6 ounces. Andrea says she just uses mayonnaise, salt and pepper on the lobster meat, but I think she either uses premium stuff or has a secret

Erica's exterior. *Photo by Sally Lerman.*

ingredient she's not telling because it really has a unique gourmet taste to it. (She does offer Kate's Butter, also from Maine and the best butter on earth, with the lobster dinners.) But perhaps she's just really skilled at cooking lobster. Either way, this spot is well worth the long drive out to Harpswell Point.

Open May through October
Cold meat with mayonnaise
Weighed in at 6 ounces

The Dolphin Marina and Restaurant

515 Basin Point Road
Harpswell, Maine 04079
207-833-6000
www.dolphinmarinaandrestaurant.com

This is certainly one of the finest views to be had while eating a lobster roll in Maine. There are other great views, but this one really just has such a peaceful, edge-of-the-world vibe. To fully take in the view, you need to have the dog greeter, black lab Louie, guide you out across the wide lawn to the end of the point, where you can see Casco Bay all around. The drive out to the very end of Harpswell Point is probably one of the main reasons that this venue is seasonal. This isn't a location that you could just stumble upon.

The Dolphin was founded in 1966 by current owner Bill Saxton's parents, Malcolm and Jean Saxton. Malcolm was going to run the marina, and Jean decided that opening up a coffee shop would be a nice idea. Over the years, that coffee shop grew into a full-service restaurant. A few years ago, the Saxtons decided to revamp

Dolphin lobster roll. *Photo by Sally Lerman.*

the layout of this prime piece of land, giving the amazing view to a new restaurant building and moving the marina and boat storage to the back. Conservation and environmentally friendly practices were a priority in the construction of the new restaurant and marina. The 2011 season was the first for what is easily the finest lobster shack in Maine. I use the term "shack" because that is how it started out. But that little shack has grown into a huge, gorgeous, full-service restaurant with floor-to-ceiling wraparound windows overlooking the bay.

But Dolphin Restaurant has stayed true to its roots. The Saxtons use only the freshest seafood and make all of their own fresh-baked goods and desserts. This is a family-run business. Bill's wife, Mimi, and their children—Maureen, Chris, Billy and Jeremy—along with daughter-in-law Maya all work together in what certainly looks like perfect harmony. Hospitality and a welcoming atmosphere are very important to them, and that is apparent from the moment you enter. They have lots of regulars who come out often, and they stay up to date on all of the goings-on. That's actually how I found out about the Dolphin. My friend Lucy's parents live in Brunswick and have been coming out here for years, and her mother highly recommended the lobster roll.

There are two lobster co-ops up the road in Harpswell where the Saxtons get all of their freshly caught Casco Bay lobsters. They cook the lobster meat in salt water, which is the key to the very best lobster meat, and they pick it in-house every day. They also use soft-shell lobsters whenever possible because they feel the meat is sweeter. I was admittedly a little jealous to find that the Saxton ladies can identify a lobster roll that uses frozen meat just by looking at it. Despite all my travels, I still need to take a bite to be sure. Then again, if I actually picked lobsters with my own hands for years, I would probably be much more attuned to what fresh picked meat looked like. The large chunks of tail, claw and knuckle meat are dressed in light mayonnaise and placed in a standard split-top bun that has been grilled to crisp perfection using real butter. It is then served with homemade potato chips.

The Dolphin really is a lobster roll experience unlike any other. It has the best parts of an authentic Maine lobster shack combined with the best of a top-quality full-service restaurant. And if all that weren't enough, it has one of the best views in Maine (certainly the best that can be enjoyed in air conditioning with a glass of wine while sitting on a real, comfortable chair). But being welcomed by a happy black dog is what really puts it into the top tier for me.

Open April through October
Cold meat with mayonnaise
Weighed in at 5.3 ounces

Grape-Nuts Custard
(recipe originated by Jean Saxton)

½ cup Grape-Nuts cereal

1 cup sugar

4 cups milk

12 eggs, beaten

2 teaspoons vanilla extract

Nutmeg

Mix Grape-Nuts, sugar and milk together in an ovenproof glass dish. Heat in microwave for seven minutes. Beat eggs and add in vanilla extract. Slowly add egg mixture into milk mixture while continually whisking. Sprinkle with nutmeg. Put dish into a hot water bath and place into 300-degree oven. Bake one hour or until the center is set.

FIVE ISLANDS LOBSTER CO.

1447 Five Islands Road
Georgetown, Maine 04548
207-371-2990
www.fiveislandslobster.com

The lobster meat at Five Islands is so good that I have actually witnessed it convert avowed non-lobster lovers. If that were the only reason to go, I would still suggest you drive from anywhere to try it. But it also has among the best views I have seen in Maine. It's called Five Islands because you can actually see five islands from the deck. I usually need assistance from someone who works there to spot all five, but it truly makes for a gorgeous vista. There is no indoor seating here, so coming on a lovely day is a more ideal experience. I once went on the last day of the season, Columbus Day, and while the lobster roll was still as fantastic as ever, it is somehow less enjoyable when you are being blown over by freezing wind and drizzle. There is one spot with a roof to protect you from the rain, but most of the green picnic tables are out in the sun, where you can watch the staff pull the lobster crates out of the water, up onto the dock and into the kitchen for cooking. You should be aware of the ordering procedure. The main building with the "Five Islands" sign on the front and "Love Nest Snack Bar" on the side is where you order the lobster roll and most other food. The building next to it is where lobster dinners are ordered, and the building across from the Love Nest is home to the ice cream. Don't ask me why it is called the Love Nest—that is one mystery I did not solve, and maybe I just don't want to.

The main building has actually been on this location for over two hundred years and has served as a fish cannery and post office, among other things. Five Islands Lobster Co. has been here for twenty-five years, and Keith Longbottom has been running it for the last eight years. In addition to being a world-class lobster eatery, it also serves as a wholesale lobster wharf, buying lobster from the forty boats that fish the area. According to Keith, this is considered one of the best lobster areas in Maine because the bottom-dwelling lobsters are caught in an area that is extremely deep—175 feet at its deepest point. I certainly can't argue with the results.

This is truly the best lobster meat I have had on a lobster roll in Maine. I don't normally make definitive statements like that. I also have trouble ranking lobster rolls and specific traits such as meat because I change my mind so frequently. But I know which ones I like more than all the others, and this is without question among the top five lobster rolls I have ever had the pleasure of eating. In fact, it's likely among the top three of the more than two hundred lobster rolls I have eaten to this

Five Islands lobster roll. *Photo by Sally Lerman.*

point. I generally consider Columbus Day weekend to be my "victory lap." It isn't for reviewing, weighing and photographing—it's just for eating. Five Islands has been a must on my victory lap each year since I first experienced it.

I think many factors converge to make this the best lobster meat to be found, but one of the big keys is freshness. The lobsters are delivered daily by the lobstermen and kept tethered in crates to the wharf in Sheepscot Bay. The crates are only pulled out when the lobsters are ready to be cooked, and they cook lobster meat for the rolls throughout the day. Just to be clear, I will say that the meat is never frozen. But the concept of frozen meat is so far from reality here that it almost seems laughable. As

Keith says, "The lobsters are never more than a few minutes out of the ocean." The lobsters for both the lobster rolls and lobster dinners are cooked in salt water, which seems to be the secret to greatness.

The meat is then torn into large chunks and allegedly tossed with a touch of mayonnaise. I say "allegedly" because you might not notice it at all, whether by looking or tasting. It just melts seamlessly into the surface of the meat, enhancing

View from Five Islands. *Photo by Sally Lerman.*

the already perfect flavor. The meat is then placed on a buttery grilled, split-top bun (dip the whole thing in melted butter if you really want to blow your mind). I also recommend getting it with onion rings. They use clam fry on their fried foods (including the fried lobster), making them better than anyone else's. There are two sizes of lobster rolls available: the regular and the "Big Boy." Personally, I see absolutely no point in ordering the regular size unless you are trying lobster for the first time. With lobster meat this good, more is always better. When I first came here, a friend noticed that I checked out the T-shirt that said "Home of the Big Boy" but didn't buy it right away. I was waiting to see if I liked the "Big Boy." I now wear that yellow shirt proudly, particularly in the winter because it reminds me of my happy place with the best lobster and a beautiful view of Maine.

Open May through October
Cold with mayonnaise
Regular weighed in at 5.0 ounces
Big Boy weighed in at 9.5 ounces

RED'S EATS

41 Water Street
Wiscasset, Maine 04578
207-882-6128

In the world of lobster roll food porn, Red's is, without a doubt, the centerfold. With its artfully curled whole tails on top and claws daintily peeking out of the ends, this is easily the prettiest lobster roll known to man. It's not just the

Red's Eats lobster roll. *Photo by Sally Lerman.*

prettiest, either; this is also the most popular, well-known lobster roll on the face of the earth.

As with anything pretty and popular, some do love to hate it. Of course, it's easy to get angry at a place that appears, at first glance, to be the cause of huge traffic jams on Route 1 during the summer. In their defense, though, I think the real cause of all that traffic is the planner who decided to run a major highway through a tiny, cute town with lots of antique shops, foot traffic and on-street parking. Certainly Red's contributes to the overall appeal of Wiscasset, but they can't be blamed for poor road planning.

I must admit that in the beginning, I was very skeptical of Red's, just as I tend to be with anything that seems overhyped or trendy. I've found so many popular places to be huge disappointments on the lobster roll front. Some, I think, are popular for reasons other than the lobster roll, such as having a great view. I'm not saying that isn't important, but the lobster roll itself should be the main attraction. I've found that other popular places—even ones that serve fresh steamed whole lobster dinners—use previously frozen meat in their lobster rolls. It gives me no pleasure to say that. I would love for every spot, particularly the popular ones, to serve a lobster roll worthy of popularity. Having eaten the Red's lobster roll quite a few times now and having had the pleasure of speaking with Debbie Gagnon, the owner, I can say that Red's is one place that lives up to the hype. It's a good feeling—kind of like finding out that the head cheerleader is actually a really kind person who saves puppies and volunteers at a soup kitchen.

I remember clearly the first time I had the Red's lobster roll. I knew that no one would trust my opinion on lobster rolls if I hadn't had this one and that if I wanted to have any accurate assessment of where the best lobster rolls were, I needed to try the one that seemed to be everyone's very favorite. To be honest, my biggest hang-up was the line. I have a personal policy of never waiting in a line that has more than three people, regardless of what I'm waiting for. Sure, there are people who love setting up camp in an overnight line, making friends in the line and turning it into a party. God bless them, but I will never be one of those people. Ironically, I will spend far more time figuring out how to get what I want without waiting in a line than just waiting would have taken.

When I finally accepted that there was no other way, I sucked it up and waited in line for an hour and twenty minutes on a ninety-degree day in July. I'd love to tell you that the line turned out to be a lot of fun, but no, waiting in line will always be terrible to me. When I finally got the lobster rolls (yes, I ordered four—I didn't wait all that time for just one), they looked even better than they had in pictures. No lover of lobster could ever possibly hold this beauty in his or her hands and say, "Meh, doesn't look worth the wait." It was everything I had dreamed of and more! Of course, being a skeptic, I then got worried that my expectations were too high. Could anything that looks that good also taste that good? The first bite made me a convert.

One of the things I get asked most is: "Doesn't all lobster meat taste the same?" Absolutely not. In my opinion, there are many tiers of lobster quality. But aside from that perfect out-of-the-sea flavor and melt-in-your-mouth tenderness, the super elite always seem to have one thing in common: tolerable spongies. This is what separates the men from the supermen. Those finger parts of the lobster claw are my least favorite part of the lobster. When a lobster roll can include them and I don't mind, we have reached lobster perfection, as achieved consistently here at Red's.

Since the building that houses Red's is somewhat smaller than some people's master bathroom, they don't cook the meat on site. Red's gets their lobster meat fresh, never frozen, every day from Atlantic Edge Lobster Co. in Boothbay Harbor or Maine Shellfish in Ellsworth. Atlantic Edge is essentially a warehouse on Boothbay Harbor that houses and cooks fresh lobsters. It is open to the public if you want to just walk in and buy some meat. They also sell and ship their fresh picked lobster meat year-round.

Another thing that makes the Red's roll different is that the meat is served unadorned. Mayonnaise or melted butter is served on the side. I always took the whole tails off the top of the buttery grilled top-split bun and dipped them in butter before eating the actual roll to make it more manageable. And after talking with Debbie, I learned that that was actually the intention. It gives the experience of eating a whole lobster combined with the experience of a lobster roll—genius!

Debbie is not actually "Red." Nor was her father, the late Al Gagnon, who purchased the defunct hot dog and hamburger stand in 1977 and turned it into the lobster roll mecca that it is today. "Red" was actually the redheaded Harold Delano, who purchased the stand in 1957. The stand has been in the same location since the 1930s. So has the elm tree on top of which the Red's back deck essentially sits. This is one of the very few remaining American elms left standing after Dutch elm disease nearly wiped out all of them in the 1940s. Debbie jokes that it's the grease that keeps it alive. You can enjoy your lobster roll on the deck under the shade of the elm or head across the street to the picnic tables overlooking Sheepscot Bay.

According to Debbie, Al got the idea of adding lobster rolls to his menu when he ate them at other places and got the "wet cardboard" taste of frozen lobster meat. That's one of the most accurate descriptions of frozen lobster meat I have heard. He wanted to do it right and "use only the freshest meat and give people plenty." They don't weigh the meat here; they simply pile it in until it looks perfect and serve it up. I actually have weighed it several times, and it comes in at about 7.5 to 8.0 ounces. They say it has more meat than one whole lobster, but considering you get about 3.0 to

Red's Eats lobster roll. *Photo by Sally Lerman.*

4.0 ounces from a 1.25-pound lobster and the weight of the Red's roll doesn't include butter or mayo, as most of my weights do, I would say this is considerably more.

The tiny woman with a smile from ear to ear who welcomes you when you finally reach the window is actually Debbie, owner and daughter of Al, inventor of the uniquely Red's version of the lobster roll. Unlike many lobster roll purveyors I spoke to in October, just before the season ended, she didn't seem the least bit tired or ready for the off-season. I sensed that sharing her joy and her father's love of the lobster roll with every person who comes to the window actually energizes her.

There are few things in this world that I would advocate waiting in line for over an hour for, but this lobster roll is one of them. Of course, I have actually figured out the secret of how to get the Red's lobster roll without waiting in much of a line. But I'm going to be shellfish and let you figure it out for yourself.

Open May through October
Cold meat with butter or mayonnaise on the side
Weighed in at 7.8 ounces

SPRAGUE'S LOBSTER

22 Main Street
Wiscasset, Maine 04578
207-882-1236

It can't be easy selling lobster rolls right across the street from the most famous lobster roll spot on earth. But you wouldn't think that after talking to Frank and Linda Sprague. These laid-back folks had nothing but nice things to say about

Sprague's lobster roll. *Photo by Sally Lerman.*

their neighbors across the street. One thing that does bother them a bit is that most tourists and journalists assume that Sprague's set up camp across the street from Red's for the sole purpose of competing against them after they became famous. I must admit that I assumed the same. In truth, the Spragues have been selling lobsters and lobster rolls in Wiscasset for the last twenty-six years. They started off on the same side of Route 1, just down at the end of the road. Then, thirteen years ago, an opportunity opened up for them to move to their current location on a deck overlooking the water. At that point, they said, Red's wasn't the attraction it is today. That didn't happen until a few years later.

Sprague's itself really has quite a lovely waterfront location. The shack is located on a wood deck where an old creamery used to stand, and it seems it's still referred to as Creamery Pier. There are a few other vendors on the pier selling arts and crafts that you can browse while waiting for your order. Sprague's is a cheery little place decorated with flowers and lots of picnic tables with bright red and white umbrellas where you can enjoy your meal while looking out directly over the peaceful Sheepscot River. The Spragues' friendly black lab hangs around the lobster cooking shack with his dad most of the day. Whole lobster dinners are a house specialty, and Frank cooks them up fresh in his kitschy little cook shack. They have fresh corn, chowder and a variety of other house-made goodies, including clam fritters. You also might want to save some room for the ice cream stand.

When it comes to their lobster roll, the Spragues stick to what their customers like, not necessarily what they prefer. Frank really likes his lobster meat chopped into small pieces with a generous amount of mayonnaise, but he knows that's not how visitors like it. The Spragues use a standard split-top hot dog bun, crisp and buttery grilled on the sides. It nearly broke my heart when Linda told me that when they tried using bakery-fresh buns, they got so many complaints that they had to go back to the standard grocery store–type bun.

They use only fresh picked Maine lobster meat, delivered fresh every day by Atlantic Edge Lobster Co. in Boothbay. Atlantic Edge Lobster Co. really does make some of the most superior lobster meat I have had the pleasure of eating. I don't know what their secret is, but their meat is absolute lobster perfection. And they manage to achieve a near impossible feat for their lobster meat: the spongies (claw fingers) have a texture that I actually enjoy. They are not the slightest bit tough and melt seamlessly into the rest of the meat.

Sprague's keeps the chunks of tail meat very large but not whole. They do leave the claws whole. They then toss the meat with a "scant amount" of mayonnaise and serve. Since they're made to order, you can request more mayo, no mayo or butter

Frank Sprague of Sprague's Lobster. *Photo by Sally Lerman.*

on the side. Sprague's lobster roll weighs in at 7 ounces. Sprague's is worth a trip in itself, but if that's not in the cards, and you are waiting in the Red's line, I strongly suggest you send someone in your party across the street to sample the fabulousness of the Sprague's lobster roll as well and bring one back.

Open May through October
Cold meat with mayonnaise
Weighed in at 7 ounces

BOOTHBAY LOBSTER WHARF

97 Atlantic Avenue
Boothbay Harbor, Maine 04538
207-633-4900
www.boothbaylobsterwharf.com

This is *the* best place in New England to get that authentic lobster roll experience. There are other places where you will find an amazingly fresh lobster roll, a gorgeous view, comfortable indoor and outdoor seating, entertainment and a full bar or extensive menu. But this is the only place I have ever found that has it all wrapped up in a decidedly festive atmosphere. Boothbay Lobster Wharf literally has it all.

I suspect that owner Todd Simmons's business philosophy is that he is throwing a party every night and all are invited. On most weekends, there is a different band rocking it out on the outdoor deck playing a wide variety of music genres. You'll find couples, old and young, dancing the night away by the picnic tables; dogs hanging

Boothbay Lobster Wharf lobster roll. *Photo by Sally Lerman.*

out with their owners and making friends; kids watching the lobster boats being unloaded; and tables of people who were complete strangers ten minutes before chatting it up and exchanging stories about the best whale-watching tours they found. The fun continues nonstop from Memorial Day to Columbus Day.

Presiding over it all is Todd, who exudes the relaxed vibe of a man who just got off work on a Friday night even though he is, in fact, running a very busy restaurant. Maybe it comes from the fact that he was a lobsterman for most of his life, having given it up only recently. Lobstering is a far more difficult job than some realize. It involves waking up long before the sun to head out on the possibly treacherous

Boothbay Lobster Wharf's Todd Simmons. *Photo by Sally Lerman.*

ocean and haul in traps all day long—many of which will come up with nothing that you can keep. So for Todd, perhaps owning a fabulous harbor-side lobster restaurant is just that: Friday night. Todd purchased what is now Boothbay Lobster Wharf (BLW) from a Lobster Co-op restaurant that was here before. He made a few changes to the menu, but BLW remains as it has been for thirty years: a working wharf where fishermen and lobstermen unload their fresh catch daily. Lobster wharf–owned lobster roll establishments are rather elusive, and those owned by an actual lobsterman are even more rare.

Boothbay Lobster Wharf is the very favorite lobster roll place of every member of my family, and I have taken them to all of my top spots. This lobster roll is, without question, one of my very favorites anywhere. But it's more than just that. This is the place that gets me through the long, cold Columbus–Memorial Day season. Perhaps that's why I always stay in Boothbay Harbor for the Columbus Day victory lap. I might have mentioned it before, but the victory lap weekend is when I figure out the lobster rolls that I really love. As I'm rather bad at ranking, I never really figure out which lobster rolls are my favorites until I map out the weekend and know which ones I just can't miss. I'm not visiting any new places on Columbus Day weekend. I'm not taking any notes or photos or doing any reviews. This trip is purely for pleasure. It's kind of like a reward for trying all the lesser lobster rolls I happen upon throughout the season. There are no disappointments—only the best. I would say that I usually visit BLW a minimum of four times in a Columbus Day weekend. Picturing myself sitting on that deck in the sun, watching the boats go by, sipping a Boothbay Sunset cocktail and stuffing myself with that giant lobster roll is my happy place.

I've heard many people say that one lobster roll or another is the biggest anywhere. They are wrong. It's easy to look at a roll and say it's the biggest. But looks are deceiving. I have weighed all the ones I have ever heard mentioned, and this one is the champ. This is the very largest standard-sized lobster roll available anywhere, weighing in consistently at over 10 ounces and usually over 11. If that weren't enough, they also offer a jumbo lobster roll that weighs in at over 15 ounces, though I actually think two standard-size rolls might be the better deal meat-wise. BLW uses all fresh picked meat. Their lobsters are purchased every day right on the wharf, cooked every night in seawater and picked fresh every morning. Seawater is the secret of the best-tasting lobster rolls. Lobster was meant to taste like the sea; cooking them in fresh water washes that away. When I tell Todd his lobster roll is the largest I have ever weighed, he

Boothbay Lobster Wharf exterior. *Photo by Sally Lerman.*

chuckles and says that he doubts he makes any money on the lobster rolls. He just likes to fill it "good and full of meat." I'm afraid I have to agree about his likely profit margin. But if he ever changes anything, I hope it's the price and not this sweet, tasty giant.

As with many of the great lobster rolls of Maine, this lobster roll generally uses soft-shell lobster meat. It seems that nearly every lobster purveyor I asked prefers soft shell, but Todd had a slightly different answer. He prefers lobsters caught in September and October, when the soft shells are beginning to harden. This gives you the best of both worlds. The BLW lobster roll includes the holy grail for me: uncut tail meat. Some, thinking that the whole thing will come out in one bite, scoff at the idea. But not if it's cooked right—it will be so tender that your teeth will be the only knife you need. I've counted up to five half tails (tails are split down the middle to devein) in a standard lobster roll and an abundance of whole claws and knuckles mixed with a minimal amount of mayonnaise. Each roll is mixed to order, so if you prefer it naked or with butter on the side, just say so. The meat is placed in a standard top-split bun buttery grilled to perfection. The jumbo comes in a steak-style roll, buttery grilled inside. You can even get the fresh meat on a salad if you're feeling health conscious. I tried that once, but I ended up dipping the meat in butter and mostly skipping the greens. I find the best way to enjoy this beauty is with mayo and dipped in butter. Calorie-counting is for the winter!

I happen to think that this is the most undiscovered gem in the lobster roll world. Despite the fact that it is always busy here, for some strange reason, I don't see it on the yearly "best of" lists that come out in publications like *Down East*, *Yankee* and *Boston* magazines and newspapers. Even most of the bloggers don't seem turned on to this. Part of me really hates to share this paragon of lobster roll experience perfection with the world. But it just wouldn't be fair for me to keep the secret of the finest lobster summer destination to myself.

Open May through October
Cold meat with mayonnaise, butter or neither
Regular size weighed in at 11.5 ounces
Jumbo weighed in at 15.1 ounces

MUSCONGUS BAY LOBSTER CO.

28 Town Landing Road
Round Pond, Maine 04564
207-529-5528
www.mainefreshlobster.com

The bun used at Muscongus might be one of my favorites used anywhere. Its fresh-baked goodness can best be described as tasting like it just came out of mom's oven—well, my mom's. I was the only kid in the '70s getting her sandwich on wheat bread, a joy that I didn't fully appreciate then. For me, the bun is the most underrated component of a world-class lobster roll. Muscongus, while staying true to the concept of the buttery grilled top-split bun, takes a more artisan approach. This bun is truly worthy of lobster meat so fresh that you can watch it being delivered on the docks while you savor the deliciousness. You have your choice of white or wheat, and there is no wrong choice. But don't even try to find the bakery that makes these buns. They're actually homemade and delivered fresh every day by a friend of the owners, Andrea and Dan Reny.

Muscongus lobster roll. *Photo by Sally Lerman.*

The bun is so amazing that you might overlook the freshness of the actual lobster meat. They use soft-shell lobsters that are fished right out of Muscongus Bay and then delivered straight from the lobstermen to Muscongus Bay Lobster Co.—no middleman involved. This is one of the few places where the lobster chain stops right at the lobster wharf, allowing Muscongus Bay Lobster Co. to create one of the freshest lobster rolls to be found.

As if the perfect bun and fresh meat weren't enough, Muscongus is situated on one of the most peaceful spots in Maine. People bring their coolers, wine, sides and tablecloths and set up camp for the evening at one of the picnic tables overlooking the bay. Dan's grandfather Robert Reny, the founder of the Reny's department stores, found throughout Maine, started Muscongus Bay Lobster Co. in 1969 with a friend. In 2002, Dan gave up working in aquaculture growing oysters and took over the family business from his uncle Mike Reny. Dan decided to construct a new building that would allow him to have a full kitchen and use his culinary skills to expand the menu. Dan and Andrea run the business from a tiny one-room building on the other end of the pier. What it lacks in space, it more than makes up for in view.

A great lobster roll should be a combo of meat and bread so fresh and fantastic that it can be enjoyed only on that day and in that location by the sea. This one nailed all three—a major rarity in the lobster roll world.

Open May through October
Cold meat with mayonnaise
Weighed in at 8.2 ounces

MILLER'S LOBSTER COMPANY

83 Eagle Quarry Road
Spruce Head, Maine 04859
207-594-7406
www.millerslobster.com

It had taken me quite some time to make it to Miller's, despite the fact that it has been on my "to visit" list from the beginning. I think that's because Miller's is a member of the ten-week club—a group of lobster roll venues that are open only from mid-June to Labor Day. I've found that members of this club are usually

Miller's lobster roll. *Photo by Sally Lerman.*

some of the best, and Miller's is no exception. It's not that I don't like Maine in summer—well, maybe it is. I'm really more of a shoulder season person; heat and crowds just aren't my thing. But I braved it last summer to accomplish my mission of hunting down the elusive Miller's lobster roll at long last.

I was very excited when I arrived. I had waited a long time for this moment. Miller's is right on the water and offers a gorgeous view of Wheeler Bay. They have a deck with bright red picnic tables surrounded on three sides by water, where you can watch the lobster boats unload their catch while you enjoy your food. Part of the seating area is shaded by a pavilion. When I entered, I noticed a sign stating that they were no longer BYOB. I imagine many are disappointed about that, but I was thrilled. I never can seem to get it together enough to remember to bring wine with me. And they have developed quite an impressive list of wines by the glass, with many varieties and regions represented. I feel safe

View from Miller's. *Photo by Sally Lerman.*

in saying that it's likely the finest wine list for a place that serves wine in a plastic cup at a picnic table.

Miller's was started in 1977 by Luther Miller and his son Steve Miller. Steve's son Mark and his wife, Gail, have owned it since 1992. The Millers actually use their own boats to go out and catch the lobster, so you know this is some fresh stuff. I always like to see as few middlemen as possible involved in lobster roll production. The menu is simple, offering lobster, some chowders, lobster rolls, a few sides and daily pie specials. For the lobster roll, they cook and pick the meat every day and don't mix it with anything until you order. They tear the cold tail, claw and knuckle meat into huge chunks and mix it with the tiniest bit of Miracle Whip. I know some aren't fans of Miracle Whip, but I find that its sweetness works well with lobster meat when used sparingly. If you ask, they will serve the roll plain with butter on the side. Or you could do what I do and get it with the Miracle Whip *and* dip it in the butter—the best of both worlds. They use a top-split, buttery grilled bun here. The bun philosophy at Miller's is to use as little bread as possible. I think they're spot on with that philosophy. Any time you tip the meat-to-bread ratio in favor of meat, people are usually happy. The lobster roll weighed in at 6 ounces but looked more overstuffed than its weight would indicate. The flavor was fantastic and briny—everything you would expect from a place that hauls up their own lobsters right to the kitchen every day.

Open June through September
Cold with mayonnaise
Weighed in at 6 ounces

Young's Lobster Pound

2 Fairview Street
Belfast, Maine 04915
207-338-1160
www.youngslobsterpound.webs.com

Young's has been in business for eighty-three years now. Raymond Young is the third generation of the Young family to own the business. Historically, the Youngs have been lobstermen, but they have since gotten out of the actual lobstering profession. Now they simply buy and store lobsters in their massive tank system—a huge building filled with stacked tanks full of live lobsters, creating a pleasant but loud hum when you walk in. The majority of the seating is located on the second floor and is enclosed and heated. There is also outdoor seating on the first and second floors, as well as a pretty view of the Passagassawakeag River. Don't ask me how that extravagant name is pronounced—I have no idea.

When you come in, you are greeted by the extraordinarily friendly folks Raymond has working here. I'm not usually one to care much about service or how friendly someone is. As long as I receive a tasty lobster roll in a timely manner, the mood of the person taking my order is of no matter to me. But every time I have ever gone in here, these guys are just so warm and welcoming as they guide you through the somewhat confusing ordering process. They are always more than happy to answer all your questions and, without you having to ask, even pack your to-go lobster meat on ice.

In addition to being a kitchen, Young's is first and foremost a lobster pound. They sell products such as live lobsters and handpicked lobster meat all packed up by the pound and ready for you to take home and enjoy. So even if the kitchen isn't open, you can come by any time of year and buy live lobsters or fresh picked lobster meat. Their lobster meat is some of the finest to be found. They also sell lobster tomalley

Young's lobster roll. *Photo by Sally Lerman.*

packed in convenient round plastic containers. Tomalley was always a favorite of my grandmother's, who introduced me to all things New England and especially lobster. She said it was the best part of the lobster. I can't say I'll ever come around to thinking that, though I have tried it. The tomalley is actually the lobster's liver—that green stuff you find when you break open a lobster. I asked Raymond what one might do with that much tomalley (I mean, you never find more than a teaspoon in one lobster). He said people love to use it as a dip for chips all by itself. Maybe one day I'll try it—maybe.

Even though Young's has been serving lobsters in this big red building for eighty-three years, they didn't start serving lobster rolls until the early 1980s. I've actually heard from a few longtime Maine lobster purveyors that lobster rolls became popular in these parts much later than many suspect. Young's serves a generous amount of their tail, knuckle and claw meat "naked" on a round floured bun that has been grilled on the inside. Inside the bun, they smear extra heavy mayonnaise and add a piece of lettuce. Raymond feels the secret to a great lobster roll is keeping the meat and the dressing separate until they meet in the sandwich. It allows you to really taste the meat by itself. Young's serves one of the great lobster rolls in Maine, but buying their lobster meat in the dead of winter is a favorite pastime of mine. We like to visit Acadia in the dead of winter, when nothing is open, and assembling a lobster roll right in the hotel room offers a little taste of summer.

Shop open year-round; call for restaurant hours
Cold meat with mayonnaise

Ray Young's Lobster Stew

1 pound fresh lobster meat

½ stick butter

½ teaspoon salt

½ teaspoon pepper

½ teaspoon celery seasoning

½ cup sherry

1 quart heavy cream

Sauté lobster meat in butter, salt, pepper and celery seasoning until butter turns orange. Add sherry and let steep. Add heavy cream and stir lightly. Chill and serve the next day.

CHAPTER 7

Downeast Maine

CARRIER'S MAINELY LOBSTER

10 Maine 46
Bucksport, Maine 04416
207-469-1011

I thought this place looked like a real find when I first saw a photo of the lobster roll that a friend tagged me in on Facebook. That's one of the great things about being obsessed with lobster rolls—none of my friends ever eats a lobster roll without tagging me. You can only get so many tips from Internet searches, articles, Yelp and driving around. Sometimes you just have to hear it directly from somebody who is eating at a place that has yet to be discovered by the masses. A Google search for Carrier's didn't turn up much intel, and they hadn't even broken into the double digits in Yelp reviews. But after talking to B.J. Carrier, it sounds like the discovery might have been made this past summer. You can't keep a lobster roll this fantastically fresh a secret for long. I wouldn't say Carrier's is exactly off the beaten path, but Bucksport isn't a huge destination—it's more of a stop on the way to

Carrier's lobster roll. *Photo by Sally Lerman.*

Acadia. The main reason people stop is the Fort Knox and the Penobscot Narrows Observatory, where you can take an elevator to the top of the bridge and look out over Maine. You can even see Cadillac Mountain on a clear day. Just off Route 1 is Carrier's, headquartered in the house in which B.J. Carrier grew up.

When B.J. lost his job as a salesman in the fishing community, he was looking for a new opportunity and wanted to do something to promote the guys he worked with for all those years. B.J. actually goes out regularly with the fishermen during the off-season, when Carrier's is closed. When he was considering a new career path, he decided that the lobster roll world needed lobster rolls that really tasted like fresh-out-of-the-sea lobster. "People know what Hellmann's tastes like; they want to know what lobster actually tastes like," he said. And so that became his mission—to make the freshest, most authentic lobster roll possible. As it says on his sign: "Our boats went out yesterday. We cooked and picked the lobsters this morning. Now we are making your lobster roll—'Now That's Fresh.'" Carrier's also makes a point of recognizing the lobstermen who go out every day before dawn in the potentially dangerous sea to catch these very lobsters.

B.J. much prefers soft-shell lobsters because he just doesn't think hard-shell lobsters taste as good and because the soft-shell variety have a higher salt content due to the greater volume of water in their shells. He cooks the lobsters in seawater directly from Blue Hill Bay; he never uses manufactured salt water. The water in Bucksport is too brackish for good lobster cooking. After the meat is picked, he personally mixes every batch of tail, claw and knuckle meat with the right amount of mayonnaise, which is barely, if at all, perceptible in the lobster roll. He just doesn't trust anyone else to get the amount right every time. He likes doing the quality control himself.

There are two sizes of lobster rolls available at Carrier's. The standard size includes the meat from one whole lobster, and the jumbo size has the meat of two whole lobsters. According to my weigh-in, however, I think B.J. uses considerably more than that. The standard size comes in a buttery grilled Freihoffer split-top bun, while the jumbo comes on a ten-inch roll. They will make the lobster roll any way you request. B.J. said he even had someone request mustard once—whatever makes the customer happy. The lobster rolls are served with fresh-cut french fries, meaning that when you order them, they cut a potato and drop it into the fryer at that same moment.

B.J. doesn't have much of anything in his freezer. He knows that there might be easier, less expensive ways to do things, but he's not interested. What is important to him, above all else, is to do things the right way, the freshest way. He does worry a bit about his rising popularity. He doesn't like to see much of a line because he hates to make people wait. I think he might need to get used to that because with a lobster roll this good and fresh, lobster lovers will be descending on Carrier's.

Open March through October
Cold meat with butter or mayonnaise
Jumbo weighed in at 9.6 ounces

TRENTON BRIDGE LOBSTER POUND

1237 Bar Harbor Road
Trenton, Maine 04605
207-667-2977
www.trentonbridgelobster.com

From the road, there's no mistaking what the specialty of the house is at Trenton Bridge Lobster Pound. Lobster signs and red wooden lobster cutouts cover the cheery white building with its steaming, wood-fired cooking tanks. Located on Bar Harbor Road, just before you cross the bridge onto Mount Desert Island, the Trenton Bridge Lobster Pound has remained nearly unchanged since it first started here in 1956, when George Gascon purchased it while he was finishing his career in the U.S. Navy. For ten years, George's parents ran the pound and the fish wharf they had on the Manset Shore near Southwest Harbor. George loved this business and continued to work there every day until he was eighty-nine years old. His daughter, Josette Pettegrow, now owns the business and can be found here most days along with her son Warren, the fourth generation of the family at Trenton Bridge Lobster Pound.

Trenton Bridge is open seasonally for retail and dining but serves as a year-round lobster wholesaler. While the restaurant has visually remained the same, the technology has been upgraded significantly. Josette said that Trenton Bridge is an "on-land lobster pound" and explained that originally, people did not fish off the coast of Maine in the winter but still needed to eat. Lobster pounds were dammed-off areas on the coast where many lobsters were kept and fed until the temperature dropped and they went dormant over the winter. This made lobster available year-round. The modern-day technology of on-land lobster pounds allows indoor tank environments to be maintained to keep the lobsters on a short-term basis until they are delivered to their final destination. The lobsters never stay long because they do not get fed in on-land pounds and begin to lose weight after a couple weeks.

Josette is a wealth of knowledge about all things lobster, knowledge passed down to her through the generations in the business. She feels that what makes Trenton Bridge special is the fact that it is a traditional lobster pound, not just a restaurant or a fish market. To her, that means it's a place where lobsters are stored in confinement, and you can choose your own lobster and have it weighed in front of you. Then you choose whether you would like it to be cooked, whether you want to eat in or take out and what sides you would like with your lobster. Sides include traditional lobster pound fare such as corn, chowder and desserts but nothing fried. Everything is sold separately, which allows you to pay for and receive only what you want with your lobster. Josette said that some think that in order to be considered a lobster pound, you also have to cook the lobsters in wood-fired pots filled with seawater, which they do. If you have never seen these contraptions in action, it is really quite a sight and very quintessentially Maine. Here they use six giant pots full of seawater and covered with wooden lids. The pots are enclosed in an outdoor brick oven, where wood is constantly being added to keep the fires going to boil the lobsters. The

A vintage shot of the Trenton Bridge exterior. *Photo courtesy of Trenton Bridge Lobster Pound.*

Opposite, top: Trenton Bridge lobster sandwich. *Photo by Sally Lerman.*

Opposite, bottom: Trenton Bridge's Josette and Warren Pettegrow. *Photo by Sally Lerman.*

smoke comes out of the pipes, and the steam rises all around. Trenton Bridge is one of the best places to take in this experience. You can sit in the red Adirondack chairs and watch your lobster being cooked to the right while enjoying the view of the mountains of Acadia to the left.

The lobster roll here at Trenton Bridge is, well, not a lobster roll at all but a "lobster salad sandwich." They didn't start serving the sandwich until 1979, and they wanted to serve what they and most in the region always remembered eating. The salad is composed of fresh picked lobster meat that has been chilled and mixed with some mayonnaise and finely minced celery. This is then served on sliced bakery-fresh bread, white or wheat, with a piece of fresh lettuce. The finishing flair is a garnish of a festive cherry tomato, pepper slice and cucumber lobster claw skewer. I've heard many versions of the origin of lobster-meets-bread, and they do not profess to be originators of the concept here. However, after eating this '50s-style deli sandwich–inspired combination of tender, seawater-cooked lobster meat and bakery-fresh bread, I could certainly see this as the original concept for the region.

Open May through October
Cold meat with mayonnaise

GALYN'S

17 Main Street
Bar Harbor, Maine 04609
207-288-9706
www.galynsbarharbor.com

When I come to Bar Harbor, Galyn's is my happy place—it just has such a cozy, comforting vibe. Galyn's is right on the main street running through town, and it has the most gorgeous view in all of Mount Desert Island. I happen to think that

Galyn's lobster roll. *Photo by Sally Lerman.*

Frenchman's Bay is one of the prettiest sights in the world. Otter Cliffs in Acadia is a close second, but unfortunately you won't find any lobster roll restaurants with a view of the cliffs. A great view is all well and good, but this is Maine—it's only warm enough to sit outside for maybe eight weeks out of the year. So the fact that this view can be experienced from inside a climate-controlled, full-service restaurant makes it even better. In the summer, the first floor is open to the fresh air. But the second floor has huge wraparound windows, and this is where you will find what is truly the best view of Frenchman's Bay. And although the view is amazing, I always find myself drawn back to the wood-paneled bar. This isn't the knotty pine wood paneling that can be found in most lobster roll venues; this is carved and polished mahogany "step into my library and have a brandy" paneling. Apparently, it was constructed almost entirely from material salvaged from local estates. That explains it. Galyn's has a much longer season than most places in Maine (St. Patrick's Day to Thanksgiving), which is perfect for those of us who love coming to Bar Harbor in the cold months when no one is there and we have Acadia all to ourselves.

Gail Leiser started the business back in 1986 as a place where people could get "good, not fancy, food that's well prepared and served by nice people." She nailed it. There are always friendly faces to be found here; in fact, it's usually the same faces. Gail said she has little turnover in staff, which is very unusual in the seasonal restaurant industry. What first drew me here—besides the fact that they were open in November—was that they have a lobster roll that is topped with a "homemade lobster cream." They also have a traditional mayonnaise lobster roll, but I've never tried it. I have always been of the belief that every place should offer three lobster roll options: cold with mayo, warm with butter and warm with lobster bisque. I often buy lobster bisque with my lobster rolls just so I can spoon bisque onto my roll. It is a taste delight, and Galyn's was the first place I had seen it offered as an actual menu option, not some rogue creation I make myself at the table. The Galyn's version did not disappoint. They cook and shuck lobsters fresh in-house every day to use in the lobster rolls and the lobster biscuits, which are also very good. The fresh tail, claw and knuckle meat is warmed and served in a toasted traditional top-split bun. The meat is then topped with a generous amount of the lobster cream sauce, which is thicker than a bisque but has the same flavor profile. This isn't really an easy lobster roll to eat with your hands—it's more of a fork-and-knife experience.

I strongly recommend that you end your meal with a warm bowl of Indian pudding topped with ice cream. If you've never had this old-time New England dessert, it tastes like warm gingerbread pudding—a taste sensation! Everything enjoyed in the warm, happy atmosphere of Galyn's just seems to taste a bit better than it does anywhere else.

Open March through November
Cold meat with mayonnaise or hot meat with lobster cream

Indian Pudding Recipe

1 gallon whole milk
1 cup yellow cornmeal
3¼ cups Barbados molasses
1⅓ cups light brown sugar, packed
1 tablespoon salt
2 tablespoons cinnamon
2 tablespoons dry ginger

Cook in a double boiler until thickened (it should look like it is breaking) and then bake in a two-inch hotel pan at 325 degrees for twenty to thirty minutes, until it is cracking along edges but still loose in the center.

Sawyer's Lobster Pound

465 Seawall Road
Southwest Harbor, Maine 04679
207-244-8021
www.sawyerslobsterpound.com

There is a magical little place on the far side of Mount Desert Island near the somewhat desolate Seawall. I discovered it quite accidentally. I suppose my phone has figured out that I'm usually looking for places with the word "lobster" in the name, so as I was looking up directions to somewhere else, it informed me that I was near Sawyer's Lobster Pound. Sawyer's hasn't been open very long; 2013 was only their second season. God works in mysterious ways (for me, possibly through Google Maps) because this was perhaps the find of my life. There is only one lobster roll on earth that I have found to be better, and I won't pretend that the line between first and second place isn't a very fine one. Luckily, my top two are very far away from each other—about four hours—so there is never any danger of having to decide between the two. Not that I ever would—there is always room for both.

When I first visited Sawyer's, it felt a bit like one of those dreams that materializes out of a fog in front of you and then disappears, never to return again, even though you search and search. This was no mirage, however, and I visited several times in two days. But there really is magic in this place, and it is embodied by the good witch Charlotte Gill, who runs the lobster pound with her boyfriend, a lobsterman who catches everything fresh each day. When I first asked Charlotte what makes her lobster roll great, she told me, "Love." That's all she said. Believe it or not, I had heard that before, but follow-up questions usually led to answers like a love of food, lobster, customers, etc. Not so for Charlotte. For her, love is the number-one ingredient in everything she does. She feels that when

Sawyer's lobster roll. *Photo by Sally Lerman.*

you put out that love and positive energy, it comes back to you and everyone and everything around you.

I suppose that can be best illustrated in her food, but it is also seen in her mascot and pet, Lucky the Lob-steer. Lucky is a baby cow/steer that hangs out on the lawn in front of Sawyer's with a lobster cap on, grazing in the field and posing for pictures. I actually lost some sleep that first night after I visited Sawyer's. Sure, Lucky was adorable now, but he was destined to become a hamburger one day, wasn't he? Yes, I realize the hypocrisy in saying it's okay to kill lobsters but not cows. I have no real

Sawyer's Charlotte Gill. *Photo by Sally Lerman.*

explanation. Baby cows are adorable, and lobsters look like bugs. Anyway, Charlotte was quick to clear things up for me. As it turns out, her neighbor somehow ended up with a baby cow and didn't know what to do with it. So Charlotte, an avid animal lover, adopted him. She set up a place in her yard for him to live, and he follows her around everywhere. She was looking at him one day and thought, "I think he looks like he wants to wear a T-shirt." So she put one on him, and it seemed that he did. Then she thought, "Maybe he wants to wear a lobster hat." And he seemed pretty happy about that as well. She then decided to start bringing him out to Sawyer's to hang out for the day. I was very happy to hear that the appropriately named Lucky the Lob-steer will live a long and happy life as a beloved pet.

Lucky is part of Charlotte's magical plan here. She envisions a family who has been cooped up in a car all day. The kids are going crazy, tensions are high and they are almost to their campsite. Then they see a cow wearing a raincoat and a lobster hat, and they pull over out of curiosity. Before they know it, the kids are playing with Lucky, and everyone is relaxing and enjoying a delicious dinner while listening to '50s drive-in music. All is right with the world again. For Charlotte, that's what it's all about. It's much more than just food. She wants to spread her love and make people happy. She is passionate about many things—lobster, lobster rolls, '50s-style drive-ins, animals, etc.—and she wants to bring them all together in a modern way that is uniquely her own.

And I still haven't gotten to the lobster roll. I would like to say it's the best part, but despite its status as being very tops in my book, I'm not sure. I rather think that Charlotte and her vision may be the best. This lobster roll is far better than nearly every other lobster roll I have tried. Not to be redundant, but I've tried over two hundred. The lobster meat is key. Charlotte's boyfriend catches the lobsters fresh every day, and they are cooked and on the bun the very next day. They were wild and free off the coast of Bar Harbor just yesterday. They also cook and pick lobster all day long. The first roll I ordered still had that slightly warm temperature of just-picked-moments-ago meat. She says the meat is mixed with Hellman's mayonnaise, but it was so light that

Sawyer's Lucky the Lob-steer. *Photo by Ken Lerman.*

I couldn't tell. You can also have it drizzled with butter or get the best of both worlds and order the enormous foot-long version, half with mayo and half with butter. The standard weighed in at 6.5 ounces, while the foot-long came in at 11.5 ounces.

The other key that sets this roll apart from all others is the bun, a long brioche roll that is delivered fresh every day. Charlotte cuts the sides off the bun herself so that it resembles a more traditional bun and then grills it in salted butter. She knows it costs more this way, but she feels the dense, eggy goodness is worth it.

Next season, look for more innovative and creative ideas from Charlotte, including a sundae bar, a lobster zip line down to the cooker and black-and-white movies in the evening. This woman's creativity is boundless. You won't find a place or a lobster roll like this anywhere else. And after you leave, you might think back to how wonderful it was and wonder if it was all just a dream. There are places that I consider to be my "happy places." You know—the ones you think of when you're feeling low. When someone actually creates his or her own version of a "happy place" that anyone can visit, you'll thank your "Lucky" stars it isn't a dream.

Open May through October
Cold meat with butter or mayonnaise
Regular size weighed in at 6.6 ounces
Foot-long weighed in at 11.5 ounces

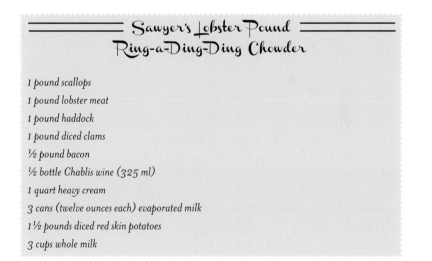

Sawyer's Lobster Pound Ring-a-Ding-Ding Chowder

1 pound scallops
1 pound lobster meat
1 pound haddock
1 pound diced clams
½ pound bacon
½ bottle Chablis wine (325 ml)
1 quart heavy cream
3 cans (twelve ounces each) evaporated milk
1½ pounds diced red skin potatoes
3 cups whole milk

3 sticks (½ cup each) salted butter

1 tablespoon dill

1 teaspoon rosemary

4 bay leaves

Combine all ingredients, leaving bacon, haddock and scallops uncooked. Cook covered in heavy-bottomed pot over medium-high heat, checking frequently, until it comes to gentle boil. Cover and simmer for another thirty to forty minutes. Remove bay leaves and enjoy. If an error is made—and if all else fails—just drink the remainder of the wine, and the soup will taste perfect.

Serves 16

ISLESFORD DOCK RESTAURANT

Islesford Dock
Islesford, Maine 04646
207-244-7494
www.islesforddock.com

Of all the lobster rolls I have tried, I would say that this one has been the most elusive. The biggest reason for this is because it's located on an island off the coast of Mount Desert Island that is accessible only by ferry. That ferry has a rather specific time schedule that allows just enough time to get dropped off on Islesford, grab some lunch and head back. If you miss that ferry, the next and last one is in

Islesford lobster roll. *Photo by Sally Lerman.*

two hours. Also, the lobster roll is served only at lunch and brunch, and that is only available Wednesday through Sunday from mid-June through Labor Day. According to my calculations, that means there are roughly only thirty days out of the year that you can get this lobster roll. But I love a challenge, and a lobster roll that plays hard to get builds that much more anticipation. Oh, I also read somewhere that Martha Stewart likes to come here—any lobster place that Martha loves must be amazing. Islesford Dock more than exceeded my already unreasonably high expectations.

The boat ride out is no picnic. It's a small boat on which more people, dogs and children than seems reasonable pack themselves in to standing-room-only levels and embark on the fairly short (thankfully) ride over. So if you have your own boat, you are obviously at a big advantage in accessing this lobster roll. When we arrive at the dock, I see Cranberry Isle Lobster Co-Op, and my excitement builds as I'm hoping that Islesford Dock uses these exotic island lobsters in their lobster roll. As it turns out, they do. I don't know why, but I suppose I was expecting a lobster roll place with the word "dock" in the name to pretty much be a takeout window on the water with a few picnic tables. Far from it, Islesford is a full-service restaurant with adorable lobster-carved chairs at the bar and lots of pleasant tables in the restaurant, which features wraparound windows overlooking the water. There must be a lot of people living on this island or all of them go there for Sunday brunch (or both) because there was actually a wait. So I headed over to the bar, took a seat in the lobster chair and ordered up a cranberry mimosa. What else would I order on the Cranberry Isles?

According to the owners, Cynthia and Daniel Lief, the dock was built in the 1800s and originally served as a coal dock. They opened their restaurant here in 1993 after a succession of previous restaurants failed. For their lobster roll, they get the lobsters exclusively from the co-op next door. They then steam and pick the lobster before each service (they never keep the lobster meat more than one day or use frozen meat). The island lobster meat was everything I hoped it could be. It was full of briny flavor and had a perfectly tender texture. The meat even had the temperature of extremely fresh picked meat—cool, not chilled. I think that is the ideal temperature at which to serve lobster meat. The meat is served on a split-top bun that has been buttered on the sides and then grilled on the kind of grill that leaves grill marks—definitely a nice touch. Cynthia says that all they use to dress the meat is "a splash of lemon, a dash of mayo and a garnish of fresh parsley or chives." But it really tasted like there was something else when I tried it. To get that light and refreshing flavor, I suspect they make their own light dressing-like mixture and just barely gloss the meat. I don't know what my obsession with the island lobsters is. I realize they come from the same water as the ones delivered to the mainland, but they just seem so much more exotic. Perhaps it's their elusive nature. You can't just run out and grab this lobster roll any time you happen to be in the area. It takes planning and effort, and you just love it when it pays off so handsomely.

Open June through September
Cold meat with mayonnaise
Weighed in at 5.5 ounces

TRACEY'S SEAFOOD

2719 U.S. 1
Sullivan, Maine 04664
207-422-9072

On Easter Sunday, Ken and I decided to venture off Mount Desert Island and head north on Route 1 to the "other" Acadia National Park: Schoodic Point (it's totally worth the trip, by the way). It felt like a really adventurous move at the time, as I had actually never been so far north on the Maine coast. I sure am glad we made the trek, because we were lucky enough to stumble upon Tracey's Seafood on Route 1, making this the northernmost lobster roll I have ever eaten. Finding a place that also served a fresh picked lobster roll was something of an Easter miracle. First, there was the sign: "$10 for a Lobster Roll and Fries." Of course, I was going to buy it either way—desperate times and all—but I immediately assumed it would be frozen

Tracey's lobster rolls. *Photo by Sally Lerman.*

meat. I almost didn't believe the gal at the order window when she said that they catch, cook and pick their own meat.

The lobster roll sure looked to be fresh and had confirmed chunks of tail, claw and knuckle meat. The standard hot dog bun was buttery grilled to perfection. It weighed in at 4.1 ounces, but remember, it was only ten dollars and came with fries. When I bit in, I immediately knew that the gal at the counter was most certainly telling the truth about this being fresh picked. It had all the briny yumminess of lobster that had been swimming in the cold waters of Maine not too long before it was in my mouth. I would have scarfed the whole thing down and told Ken to get his own had I not just stuffed myself to the brim with my favorite breakfast in Maine, blueberry pancakes from Two Cats in Bar Harbor.

On a subsequent visit much later in the season, I was able to get a behind-the-scenes tour of the lobster roll preparation, and I was truly blown away to see that what I thought was an incredible deal at Easter was now two lobster rolls for ten dollars in October. I feel very confident in saying that fresh picked lobster rolls for this price do not exist anywhere else on earth. In fact, fifteen dollars or more for one roll is pretty standard. That's why I don't normally mention price if it's in the range. This, however, is an insane steal of a deal.

The owners, Polly and Levon Tracey, started the business in 1997 as a small takeout window and have expanded since then. On a typical day, they go out lobstering for most of the day and then spend the afternoon into the evening at their processing area, cooking, picking and portioning the day's catch while making sure that there is a mix of tail, claw and knuckle meat in each. When you order your two lobster rolls, the meat is mixed to order with mayo or warmed with butter, if you prefer. It really doesn't get any fresher than a lobsterman-owned lobster roll establishment.

I like to say, "Expect nothing, and you'll never be disappointed." Some think this is a depressing view of things, but I disagree. Those who don't hold this view will never experience the unbridled joy that comes from expecting absolutely nothing and being blown away by the fabulousness of what you find. Discovering a completely unexpected, unknown, fresh picked, lobsterman-owned lobster roll this good and for this price on Easter Sunday, when the rest of Maine is closed or not carrying lobster, is pure bliss.

Open March through October
Cold meat with mayonnaise or hot with butter, upon request
Weighed in at 4.1 ounces

Side Dishes

MAIL ORDER

If you've read all this and feel super depressed because you live far from New England and don't have any upcoming trips planned, cheer up! You can have fresh picked lobster meat delivered to your door tomorrow. It isn't cheap, but it can easily be done. You can also get previously frozen meat for less money, but banish the thought if you plan to use it for lobster rolls. Here are some great places I have personally enjoyed and that ship year-round:

Atlantic Edge Lobster
71 Atlantic Avenue
Boothbay Harbor, Maine 04538
207-633-2300
866-954-2300

Hancock Gourmet Lobster Co.
www.hancockgourmetlobster.com
(Once a year, Hancock also serves a fantastic lobster roll in the Maine building at the
Eastern States Exposition, also known as "The Big E.")

James Hook and Co.
15 Northern Avenue
Boston, Massachusetts 02110
617-423-5501
www.jameshooklobster.com

Port Lobster Co.
122 Ocean Avenue
Kennebunkport, Maine 04046
207-967-2081
www.shop.portlobster.com

Index

About the Author

Sally Lerman is a gal on a quest to sample every lobster roll in New England—and maybe beyond. She has been traveling the small towns and seaside villages of New England for years in search of the best lobster rolls, having sampled them at over 225 venues, to date. This thirteenth-generation New Englander began sharing her findings with the world in 2012 through her blog, lobstergal.com. She applies her background in science, a BS in nutrition science and an MS in health promotion to her life's passion of lobster roll research, documenting the details and weighing and photographing every lobster roll she finds. She lives with her husband, Ken, in Hartford, Connecticut.

Jane Shauck Photography.

About the Photographer

Although a Midwest native, Jane Shauck met her future husband at a lobster bake on the beach in Plymouth, Massachusetts. Jane has photographed for clients such as the New York Mets, *Time* magazine, GE and Xerox, and her work has been featured in magazines such as *Real Simple*; *O, The Oprah Magazine*; *Town & Country*; and *Forbes*. She enjoys exploring the New England coast from her home in West Hartford, Connecticut, with her husband, two boys and Labrador retriever. You can view her work at www.photojane.com.